The Curious Incident of the
Dog in the Night-Time

The Curious Incident of the Dog in the Night-Time

Based on the novel by
Mark Haddon

Adapted by
Simon Stephens

Activities by
Paul Bunyan and Ruth Moore

Critical Scripts Series Editors
Paul Bunyan and Ruth Moore

Bloomsbury Methuen Drama
An imprint of Bloomsbury Publishing Plc

B L O O M S B U R Y
LONDON · OXFORD · NEW YORK · NEW DELHI · SYDNEY

Bloomsbury Methuen Drama
An imprint of Bloomsbury Publishing Plc

Imprint previously known as Methuen Drama

50 Bedford Square	1385 Broadway
London	New York
WC1B 3DP	NY 10018
UK	USA

www.bloomsbury.com

**BLOOMSBURY, METHUEN DRAMA and the Diana logo are trademarks
of Bloomsbury Publishing Plc**

This edition first published 2013
Reprinted 2013 (three times), 2014 (four times), 2015 (five times), 2016, 2017

British Library Cataloguing-in-Publication Data
A catalogue record for this book is available from the British Library.

ISBN: PB: 978-1-4081-8521-6
ePDF: 978-1-4081-8540-7
ePub: 978-1-4081-8354-0

Library of Congress Cataloging-in-Publication Data
A catalog record for this book is available from the Library of Congress

Series: Critical Scripts

Typeset by Country Setting, Kingsdown, Kent CT14 8ES
Printed and bound in Great Britain

The Curious Incident of the Dog in the Night-Time

Characters

Christopher
Siobhan
Ed, *Christopher's dad*
Mrs Alexander
Judy, *Christopher's mother*
Mrs Shears / **Voice One** / **Mrs Gascoyne** / **Woman on Train** / **Woman on Heath**
Policeman One / **Voice Two** / **Mr Thompson** / **Rhodri** / **Man behind Counter** / **Posh Man** / **Drunk Two** / **Shopkeeper** / **Roger**
Duty Sergeant / **Voice Three** / **Mr Wise** / **Uncle Terry** / **Drunk One** / **London Transport Policeman** / **Customer** / **Man on Phone**
Reverend Peters / **Voice Four** / **Station Policeman** / **Ticket Collector** / **Station Guard** / **Man with Socks** / **London Policeman** / **Ukrainian One** /
Number 44 / **Voice Five** / **Lady in Street** / **Information** / **Punk Girl** / **Ukrainian Two**

All actors remain on stage unless prescribed otherwise.

There is also a dead dog. With a fork sticking out of it.

Scenes run into one another without interruption regardless of alterations in space or time or chronology.

Part One

A dead dog lies in the middle of the stage. A large garden fork is sticking out of its side.

Christopher Boone, *fifteen years old, stands on one side of it. His forty-two-year-old neighbour* **Mrs Shears** *stands on the other.*

They stand for a while without saying anything. The rest of the company watch, waiting to see who is going to dare to speak first.

Mrs Shears   What in Christ's name have you done to my dog?

Christopher *is frozen to the spot.*

Mrs Shears   Oh no. Oh no. Oh no. Oh Christ.

Christopher's *teacher, twenty-seven-year-old* **Siobhan** *opens* **Christopher's** *book. She reads from it.*

Siobhan   It was seven minutes after midnight. The dog was lying on the grass in the middle of the lawn in front of Mrs Shears' house.

Mrs Shears   Get away from my dog.

Siobhan   Its eyes were closed. It looked as if it was running on its side, the way dogs run when they think they are chasing a cat in a dream. But the dog was not running or asleep. The dog was dead.

Mrs Shears   Get away from my dog.

Siobhan   There was a garden fork sticking out of the dog. The dog was called Wellington. It belonged to Mrs Shears who was our friend. She lived on the opposite side of the road, two houses to the left.

Mrs Shears   Get away from my dog.

Christopher *takes two steps away from the dog.*

Siobhan   My name is Christopher John Francis Boone. I know all the countries of the world and the capital cities. And every prime number up to 7507.

Mrs Shears   Get away from my dog, for Christ's sake.

Christopher *puts his hands over his ears. He closes his eyes. He rolls forward. He presses his forehead on to the grass. He starts groaning.*

Siobhan   After twelve and a half minutes a policeman arrived. He had a big orange leaf stuck to the bottom of his shoe which was poking out from one side. This is good, Christopher. It's quite exciting. I like the details. They make it more realistic.

A **Policeman** *enters. He has a big orange leaf stuck to the bottom of his shoe, which is poking out to one side. He squats next to* **Christopher**.

Siobhan   He squatted down next to me. He said to me:

Policeman One   Would you like to tell me what's going on here, young man?

Christopher *stops groaning.*

There is some time.

Christopher *lifts his head from the ground.*

There is some time.

Christopher *looks at the* **Policeman**.

There is some time.

Siobhan   I do not tell lies. Mother used to say that this was because I was a good person. But it is not because I am a good person. It is because I can't tell lies.

Christopher   The dog is dead.

Policeman One   I'd got that far.

Christopher   I think someone killed the dog.

Policeman One   How old are you?

Christopher   I'm fifteen years and three months and two days.

Policeman One   And what precisely are you doing in the garden?

Christopher   I'm talking to you.

Policeman One   Why were you in the garden in the first place?

Christopher   I could see Wellington in the garden, it looked like someone tried to plant him.

Policeman One   Did you try to plant the dog?

Christopher   No, I did not. I like dogs.

Policeman One   Did you kill the dog?

Christopher   I did not kill the dog.

Policeman One   Is this your fork?

Christopher   No.

Policeman One   You seem very upset about this.

I'm going to ask you once again.

Christopher *starts groaning.*

Policeman One   Terrific.

Christopher *carries on groaning.*

Policeman One   Young man I'm going to ask you to stop making that noise and to stand up please calmly and quietly.

Christopher *carries on groaning.*

Policeman One   Marvellous. Great. Just flipping –

The **Policeman** *tries to lift him up by his arm.*

Christopher *screams. He hits the* **Policeman**.

The **Policeman** *stares at* **Christopher**. *For a while the two look at one another, neither entirely sure what to say or quite believing what has just happened.*

Policeman One   I'm arresting you for assaulting a police officer.

I strongly advise you to get into the back of the police car because if you try any of that monkey-business again, you little shit, I am going to seriously lose my rag. Is that understood?

Siobhan   I find people confusing. This is for two main reasons. The first main reason is that people do a lot of talking without using any words. Siobhan says that if you raise one eyebrow it can mean lots of different things. It can mean 'I want to do sex with you'. I never said that.

Christopher   Yes you did.

Siobhan   I didn't use those words, Christopher.

Christopher   You did on September 12th last year. At first break.

Siobhan   And it can also mean 'I think that what you just said was very stupid'.

Duty Sergeant   Could you take your laces out of your shoes please, Christopher?

He does.

Thank you. Could you empty your pockets on to the desk please?

Christopher   Is that in case I have anything in them that I could use to kill myself or escape or attack a policeman with?

The **Duty Sergeant** *looks at him for a beat.*

Duty Sergeant   That's right.

Christopher   I've got a Swiss Army knife but I only use that for doing odd jobs not for stabbing things or hurting people.

Duty Sergeant   Jolly good.

Voice Four   A piece of string.

Voice Five   A piece of a wooden puzzle.   -

Voice Six   Three pellets of rat food for Toby, my rat.

Voice One   £1.47 (this was made up of a £1 coin, a 20p coin, two 10p coins, a 5p coin and a 2p coin).

Voice Six   A red paperclip.

Voice Four   A key for the front door.

Voice Five   A Swiss Army knife with thirteen attachments including a wire stripper and a saw and a toothpick and tweezers.

Christopher *empties his pockets.*

Duty Sergeant   Could you take your watch off please, Christopher?

Christopher   No.

Duty Sergeant   I'm sorry, Christopher?

Christopher   I need my watch to know exactly what time it is.

Duty Sergeant   Take your watch off please, Christopher.

Christopher, please will you take your watch off. I'm asking you for a final time.

Give it here, lad.

The **Duty Sergeant** *tries to take the watch.*

Christopher *starts screaming.*

The **Duty Sergeant** *stops. He moves away. He nods his head.* **Christopher** *stops screaming.*

Duty Sergeant   It's all right, son. You keep it.

Christopher *calms down.*

Duty Sergeant   Do you have any family, Christopher?

Christopher   Yes I do.

Duty Sergeant   And who is your family?

Christopher   Father and Mother but Mother's dead. And also Uncle Terry who is in Sunderland. He is my father's brother and my grandparents too but three of them are dead and Grandma Burton is in a home because she has senile dementia and thinks I'm someone on television.

Duty Sergeant   Right. Lovely. Do you know your father's phone number, Christopher?

Christopher *turns to* **Ed**. **Ed** *looks at him. He holds his hand out in front of him with his fingers stretched.*

Christopher *does the same. They touch fingers.*

Then let go.

Christopher   I could see the Milky Way as we drove towards the town centre.

Ed   Could you?

Christopher   Some people think the Milky Way is a long line of stars, but it isn't. Our galaxy is a huge disc of stars of millions of light years across and the solar system is somewhere near the outer edge of the disc.

Ed *says nothing.*

Christopher   For a long time scientists were puzzled by the fact that the sky is dark at night even though there are billions of stars in the universe and there must be stars in every direction you look, so that the sky should be full of starlight because there is very little in the way to stop the light reaching earth.

Ed *stares at him. Says nothing.*

Christopher   Then they worked out that the universe was expanding, that the stars were all rushing away from one another after the Big Bang and the further the stars were away from us the faster they were moving, some of them nearly as fast as the speed of light, which was why their light never reached us.

Ed Is that right?

Christopher And when the universe has finished exploding all the stars will slow down, like a ball that has been thrown into the air and they will come to a halt and they will all begin to fall towards the centre of the universe again. And then there will be nothing to stop us seeing all the stars in the world because they will all be moving towards us, gradually faster and faster and we will know that the world is going to end soon because when we look up into the sky at night there will be no darkness, just the blazing light of billions and billions of stars, all falling.

Ed Terrific.

Duty Sergeant Christopher. Mr Boone. Could you come this way please?

Christopher Are you going to interview me and record the interview?

Duty Sergeant I don't think there will be any need for that.

I've spoken to your father and he says you didn't mean to hit the policeman.

Did you mean to hit the policeman?

Christopher Yes.

Duty Sergeant But you didn't mean to hurt the policeman?

Christopher No. I didn't mean to hurt the policeman, I just wanted him to stop touching me.

Duty Sergeant You know that it's wrong to hit a policeman don't you?

Christopher I do.

Duty Sergeant   Did you kill the dog, Christopher?

Christopher   I didn't kill the dog.

Duty Sergeant   Do you know that it is wrong to lie to a policeman and that you can get into a very great deal of trouble if you do?

Christopher   Yes.

Duty Sergeant   Do you know who killed the dog?

Christopher   No.

Duty Sergeant   Are you telling the truth?

Christopher   Yes. I always tell the truth.

Duty Sergeant   Right. I'm going to give you a caution.

Christopher   Is that going to be on a piece of paper like a certificate I can keep?

Duty Sergeant   No. A caution means that we are going to keep a record of what you did, that you hit a policeman but that it was an accident and that you didn't mean to hurt the policeman.

Christopher   But it wasn't an accident.

Ed   Christopher, please.

Duty Sergeant   If you get into any more trouble we will take out this record and see that you have been given a caution and we will take things much more seriously. Do you understand what I'm saying?

Christopher   Yes.

Siobhan   The second main reason is that people often talk using metaphors. These are examples of metaphors:

Voice One   I am going to seriously lose my rag.

Voice Two   He was the apple of her eye.

Voice Three   They had a skeleton in the cupboard.

Voice Four   We had a real pig of a day.

Voice Five   The dog was stone dead.

Siobhan   The word metaphor means carrying something
from one place to another and it is when you describe
something by using a word for something that it isn't. This
means that the word metaphor is a metaphor. Sorry?
This means that the word metaphor is a metaphor. Wow.
That's clever.

Christopher   It's true.

Siobhan   Yes. I think it should be called a lie because a pig
is not like a day and people do not have skeletons in their
cupboards. And when I try and make a picture of the phrase
in my head it just confuses me because imagining an apple
in someone's eye doesn't have anything to do with liking
someone a lot and it makes you forget what the person was
talking about.

Christopher *turns to* **Ed**.

Christopher   I'm sorry.

Ed   It's OK.

Christopher   I didn't kill the dog.

Ed   I know.

Christopher, you have to stay out of trouble, OK?

Christopher   I didn't know I was going to get into trouble.
I like Wellington and I went to say hello to him, but I didn't
know that someone had killed him.

Ed   Just try and keep your nose out of other people's
business.

Christopher   I am going to find out who killed Wellington.

Ed   Were you listening to what I was saying, Christopher?

Christopher   Yes, I was listening to what you were saying but when someone gets murdered you have to find out who did it so that they then can be punished.

Ed   It's a bloody dog, Christopher, a bloody dog.

Christopher   I think dogs are important too.

Ed   Leave it.

Christopher   I wonder if the police will find out who killed him and punish the person.

Ed   I said leave it, for God's sake.

Christopher   Are you sad about Wellington?

Ed   Yes, Christopher, you could say that. You could very well say that.

Siobhan *reads more from the book.*

Siobhan   Mother died two years ago.

I came home from school one day and no one answered the door, so I went and found the secret key that we keep under a flowerpot outside the kitchen window. I let myself into the house and wiped my feet on the mat. I put my keys in the bowl on the table. I took my coat off and hung by the side of the fridge so it would be ready for school the next day and gave three pellets of rat food to Toby who is my pet rat. I made myself a raspberry milkshake and heated it up in the microwave. Then I went up to my bedroom and turned on my bedroom light and played six games of Tetris and got to level 38 which is my fourth best ever score. An hour later Father came home from work.

Ed   Christopher, have you seen your mum?

Christopher   No.

Siobhan   He went downstairs and started making some phone calls. I did not hear what he said. Then he came up to my room and said he had to go out for a while and he wasn't sure how long he would be. He said that if I needed anything I should call him on his mobile phone.

Some of the company look at **Siobhan** *or* **Christopher** *or* **Ed** *waiting to find out what happens next.*

Siobhan   He was away for two and a half hours. When he came back I went downstairs.

Other characters watch **Christopher** *as he approaches* **Ed***.*

Ed *doesn't look at* **Christopher***. There is some time before* **Ed** *speaks.*

Ed   I'm afraid you won't be seeing your mother for a while.

Christopher   Why not?

Ed   Your mother has had to go into hospital.

Christopher   Can we visit her?

Ed   No.

Christopher   Why can't we?

Ed   She needs rest. She needs to be on her own.

Christopher   Is it a psychiatric hospital?

Ed   No. It's an ordinary hospital. She has a problem . . . a problem with her heart.

Christopher   We will need to take food to her.

Ed   I'll take some to her during the day when you're at school and I'll give it to the doctors and they can give it to your mum, OK?

Christopher   But you can't cook.

Ed   Christopher. Look. I'll buy some ready-made stuff from Marks and Spencer's and take those in. She likes those.

Christopher   I'll make her a get-well card.

If I make her a get-well card will you take it in for her tomorrow?

Siobhan   How are you today, Christopher?

Christopher   I'm very well, thank you.

Siobhan   That's good.

Christopher   In the bus on the way to school we passed four red cars in a row.

Siobhan   Four?

Christopher   So today is a Good Day.

Siobhan   Great. I am glad.

Christopher   I've decided I am going to try and find out who killed Wellington because a Good Day is a day for projects and planning things.

Siobhan   Who's Wellington?

Christopher   Wellington is a dog that used to belong to my neighbour Mrs Shears who is our friend but he is dead now because somebody killed him by putting a garden fork through him. And I found him and then a policeman thought I'd killed him but I hadn't and then he tried to touch me so I hit him and then I had to go to the police station.

Siobhan   Gosh.

Christopher   And I am going to find out who really killed Wellington and make it a project. Even though Father told me not to.

Siobhan   Did he?

Christopher   Yes.

Siobhan   I see.

Christopher   I don't always do what I'm told.

Siobhan   Why?

Cl... cause when people tell you what to do it is
...nd does not make sense. For example,
...e quiet' but they don't tell you how long

...ny did your father tell you not to try to find
...llington, Christopher?

...on't know.

...opher, if your father's told you not to do
...e you shouldn't do it.

...it to be writing stories today, so why don't
...what happened to you last night?

...K I will.

...help you.

...Vill you help me with the spelling and the
g...ie footnotes?

Ed Christopher, I'm sorry, your mother's died.

She's had a heart attack.

It wasn't expected.

Christopher   What kind of heart attack?

Ed   I don't know what kind of heart attack. Now isn't the moment, Christopher, to be asking questions like that.

Christopher   It was probably an aneurysm.

Ed   I'm sorry, Christopher, I'm really sorry.

A form representing Christopher's street is assembled.

Siobhan   That evening I went round to Mrs Shears' house and knocked on the door and waited for her to answer it.

Mrs Shears *answers her door. She is drinking a cup of tea.*

Mrs Shears   What are you doing here?

Christopher   I wanted to come and tell you that I didn't kill Wellington. And also I want to find out who killed him.

Mrs Shears   Christopher, I really don't think I want to see you right now.

Christopher   Do you know who killed Wellington?

Mrs Shears   Can you go now, Christopher.

Christopher   I wanted to see if the fork was in the shed.

Mrs Shears   If you don't go now I will call the police again.

Christopher   Reverend Peters, where is heaven?

Reverend Peters   I'm sorry, Christopher?

Christopher   In our universe whereabouts is it exactly?

Reverend Peters   It's not in our universe. It's another kind of place altogether.

Christopher   There isn't anything outside our universe, Reverend Peters. There isn't another kind of place altogether. Except there might be if you go through a Black Hole. But a Black Hole is what is called a Singularity which means it's impossible to find out what is on the other side because the gravity of a Black Hole is so big that even electromagnetic waves like light can't get out of it, and electromagnetic waves are how we get information about things which are far away. And if heaven is on the other side of a Black Hole then dead people would have to be fired into space on a rocket to get there and they aren't or people would notice.

Reverend Peters *looks at him for a while before he responds.*

Reverend Peters   Well when I say heaven is outside our universe it's really just a manner of speaking. I suppose what it really means is that they are with God.

Christopher   But where is God?

Reverend Peters   Christopher, we should talk about this on another day when I have more time.

Siobhan   The next day was Saturday and there is not much to do on a Saturday unless Father takes me out somewhere on an outing to the boating lake or to the garden centre, but on this Saturday England were playing Romania at football which meant that we weren't going to go on an outing because Father wanted to watch the match on the television. So I made a decision. I decided to do some more detection. I decided to go out on my own.

Mr Thompson   Can I help you?

Christopher   Do you know who killed Wellington?

Mr Thompson   Who are you?

Christopher   I'm Christopher Boone from number 36 and I know you. You're Mr Thompson.

Mr Thompson   I'm Mr Thompson's brother.

Christopher   Do you know who killed Wellington?

Mr Thompson   Who the hell is Wellington?

Christopher   Mrs Shears' dog. Mrs Shears is from number 41.

Mr Thompson   Someone killed her dog?

Christopher   With a fork.

Mr Thompson   Jesus Christ.

Christopher   A garden fork. Do you know who killed him?

Mr Thompson   I haven't a bloody clue.

Christopher   Did you see anything suspicious on Thursday evening?

Mr Thompson   Look son, do you really think you should be going round asking questions like this?

Christopher   Yes, because I want to find out who killed Wellington and I am writing a book about it.

Mr Thompson   Well, I was in Colchester on Thursday so you're asking the wrong bloke.

Christopher   Thank you.

Number 44   It's Christopher isn't it?

Christopher   Yes it is. Do you know who killed Wellington?

Number 44   No. No. I don't. No. I'm sorry.

Christopher   Did you see anything suspicious on Thursday evening, which might be a clue?

Number 44   Like what?

Christopher   Like strangers or the sound of people arguing.

Number 44   I didn't, Christopher, no.

Christopher   Do you know of anyone who might want to make Mrs Shears sad?

Number 44   Perhaps you should be talking to your father about this.

Christopher   I can't talk to my father about it because he told me to stay out of other people's business.

Number 44   Well maybe he has a point, Christopher.

Christopher   So you don't know anything that might be a clue?

Number 44   No. You be careful, young man.

Christopher   I will be. Thank you for helping me with my questions.

Do you know who killed Wellington on Thursday night?

Mr Wise   Bloody hell. Policemen really are getting younger, aren't they?

Mr Wise *laughs.* **Christopher** *walks away.*

Christopher   Do you know anything about Wellington getting killed?

Mrs Alexander   I'm afraid you're going to have to say that again. I'm a little deaf.

Christopher   Do you know anything about Wellington getting killed?

Mrs Alexander   I heard about it yesterday. Dreadful. Dreadful.

Christopher   Do you know who killed him?

Mrs Alexander   No, I don't.

Christopher   Somebody must know because the person who killed Wellington knows that they killed Wellington. Unless they were a mad person and didn't know what they were doing. Or unless they had amnesia.

Mrs Alexander   Well, I suppose you're probably right.

Christopher   Thank you for helping me with my investigation.

Mrs Alexander   You're Christopher, aren't you?

Christopher   Yes. I live at number 36.

Mrs Alexander   We haven't talked before, have we?

Christopher   No. I don't talk to strangers. But I'm doing detective work.

Mrs Alexander   I see you every day, going to school. It's very nice of you to come and say hello. Even if it's only because you're doing detective work.

Christopher   Thank you.

Mrs Alexander   I have a grandson your age.

Christopher   My age is fifteen years and three months and three days.

Mrs Alexander   Well, almost your age. You don't have a dog, do you?

Christopher   No.

Mrs Alexander   You'd probably like a dog, wouldn't you?

Christopher   I have a rat.

Mrs Alexander   A rat?

Christopher   He's called Toby.

Mrs Alexander   Oh.

Christopher   Most people don't like rats because they think they carry diseases like bubonic plague. But that's only because they lived in sewers and stowed away on ships coming from foreign countries where there were strange diseases. But rats are very clean.

Mrs Alexander   Do you want to come in for tea?

Christopher   I don't go into other people's houses.

Mrs Alexander   Well maybe I could bring some tea out here. Do you like lemon squash?

Christopher   I only like orange squash.

Mrs Alexander   Luckily I have some of that as well. And what about Battenberg?

Christopher   I don't know because I don't know what Battenberg is.

Mrs Alexander   It's a kind of cake. It has marzipan icing round the edge.

Christopher   Is it a long cake with a square cross-section which is divided into equally sized, alternately coloured squares.

Mrs Alexander   Yes, I think you could probably describe it like that.

Christopher   I think I'd like the pink squares but not the yellow squares because I don't like yellow. And I don't know what marzipan is so I don't know whether I'll like that.

Mrs Alexander   I'm afraid marzipan is yellow too.
Perhaps I should bring out some biscuits instead. Do you
like biscuits?

Christopher   Yes. Some sorts of biscuits.

Mrs Alexander   I'll get a selection.

She goes into her house.

He waits. Then before she gets back.

Siobhan   She moved very slowly because she was an old
lady and she was inside the house for more than six minutes
and I began to get nervous because I didn't know her well
enough to know whether she was telling the truth about
getting orange squash and Battenberg cake. And I thought
she might be ringing the police and then I'd get into
much more serious trouble because of the caution. So I
walked away.

Christopher   Why would you kill a dog?

Siobhan   I wouldn't.

Christopher   I think you would only kill a dog if a) you
hated the dog or b) if you were mad or c) because you
wanted to make Mrs Shears upset. I don't know anybody
who hated Wellington so if it was a) it was probably a
stranger. I don't know any mad people either, so if it was b) it
was also probably a stranger.

Siobhan   Right.

Christopher   But most murders are committed by
someone who is known to the victim. In fact, you are most
likely to be murdered by a member of your own family on
Christmas Day.

Siobhan   Is that a fact?

Christopher   Yes actually it is a fact. Wellington was
therefore most likely to have been killed by someone known
to him. I only know one person who didn't like Mrs Shears

and that is Mr Shears who divorced Mrs Shears and left her to live somewhere else and who knew Wellington very well indeed. This means that Mr Shears is my Prime Suspect.

Siobhan   Christopher.

Christopher   I am going to find out more about Mr Shears.

Mrs Gascoyne   Mr Boone, nobody has ever taken an A-Level in the school before.

Ed   He can be the first then.

Mrs Gascoyne   I don't know if we have the facilities in the school to allow him to do that.

Ed   Then get the facilities.

Mrs Gascoyne   I can't treat Christopher differently to any other student.

Ed   Why not?

Mrs Gascoyne   Because then everybody would want to be treated differently.

Ed   So?

Mrs Gascoyne   It would set a precedent. Christopher can always do his A-Levels later. When he's eighteen.

Ed   Christopher is getting a crap enough deal already, don't you think, without you shitting on him from a great height as well. Jesus, this is the one thing he's really good at.

Mrs Gascoyne   We should talk about this later. Maybe on our own.

Ed   Are there things which you're too embarrassed to say to me in front of Christopher?

Mrs Gascoyne   No. It's not that.

Ed   Say them now then.

Mrs Gascoyne   If Christopher sits an A-Level then he would have to have a member of staff looking after him on his own in a separate room.

Ed   I'll pay for it. They can do it after school. Here. Fifty quid. Is that enough?

Mrs Gascoyne   Mr Boone.

Ed   I'm not going to take no for an answer.

Ed *turns to* **Christopher**.

Ed   Where have you been?

Christopher   I have been out.

Ed   I have just had a phone call from Mrs Shears. What the hell were you doing poking round her garden?

Christopher   I was doing detective work trying to figure out who killed Wellington.

Ed   How many times do I have to tell you, Christopher? I told you to keep your nose out of other people's business.

Christopher   I think Mr Shears probably killed Wellington.

Ed (*shouts*)   I will not have that man's name mentioned in my house.

Beat.

Everybody on stage pauses to look at **Ed** *and* **Christopher**.

Christopher   Why not?

Ed   That man is evil.

Christopher   Does that mean he might have killed Wellington?

Ed   Jesus wept.

Christopher   I know you told me not to get involved in other people's business but Mrs Shears is a friend of ours.

Ed   Well, she's not a friend any more.

Christopher   Why not?

Ed   OK Christopher. I am going to say this for the last and final time. I will not tell you again. Look at me when I'm talking to you, for God's sake. Look at me. You are not to go asking Mrs Shears who killed that bloody dog. You are not to go asking anyone who killed that bloody dog. You are not to go trespassing on other people's gardens. You are to stop this ridiculous bloody detective game right now. I am going to make you promise me, Christopher. And you know what it means when I make you promise.

Christopher   I know.

Ed   Promise me that you will give up this ridiculous game right now, OK?

Christopher   I promise.

Siobhan   I think I would make a very good astronaut.

Ed   Yes mate. You probably would.

Siobhan   To be a good astronaut you have to be intelligent and I'm intelligent. You also have to understand how machines work and I'm good at understanding how machines work.

Christopher   You also have to be someone who would like being on their own in a tiny spacecraft thousands and thousands of miles away from the surface of the earth and not panic or get claustrophobia or homesick or insane. And I really like little spaces so long as there is no one else in them with me.

Ed   I noticed.

Siobhan   Sometimes when I want to be on my own I get into the airing cupboard and slide in beside the boiler and pull the door closed behind me and sit there and think for hours and it makes me feel very calm.

Christopher   So I would have to be an astronaut on my own or have my own part of the spacecraft that no one else could come into. And also there are no yellow things or brown things in a spacecraft so that would be OK, too.

And I would have to talk to other people from Mission Control, but we would do that through a radio link-up and a TV monitor so it wouldn't be like real people who are strangers but it would be like playing a computer game.

Ed   Which you like.

Christopher   Also I wouldn't be homesick at all because I'd be surrounded by lots of things I like, which are machines and computers and outer space. And I would be able to look out of a little window in the spacecraft and know that there was no one else near me for thousands and thousands –

Ed   Christopher.

Christopher   What?

Ed   Could you please, just, give it a bit of a break, mate. Please.

The two look at each other.

Siobhan   And know that there was no one else near me for thousands and thousands of miles which is what I sometimes pretend at night in the summer when I go and lie on the lawn and look up at the sky and I put my hands round the sides of my face so that I can't see the fence and the chimney and the washing line and I can pretend I'm in space.

And all I could see would be stars. And stars are the places where the molecules that life is made of were constructed billions of years ago. For example, all the iron in your blood, which stops you being anaemic, was made in a star.

And I would like it if I could take Toby with me into space, and that might be allowed because they sometimes do take animals into space for experiments, so if I could think of a good experiment you could do with a rat that didn't hurt the rat, I could make them let me take Toby.

But if they didn't let me I would still go because it would be a Dream Come True.

Christopher   Father said.

Siobhan   I see, that's a pity.

Christopher   So the book is finished.

Siobhan   Well, Christopher, if your father said he wanted you to stop then I think he probably has a good reason and I think you should stop. But you can still be very proud because what you've written so far is just, well it's great.

Christopher   It's very short.

Siobhan   Well, some very good books are very short.

Christopher   Like what?

Siobhan   Like, like *Heart of Darkness*.

Christopher   Who wrote *Heart of Darkness*?

Siobhan   Joseph Conrad.

Christopher   Did you like my diagram of the universe?

Siobhan   I did. Very much.

Christopher   And the map of the street. Which is accurate. And the way the chapters are all prime numbers.

Siobhan   I noticed that.

Christopher   It's not a proper book.

Siobhan   Why not?

Christopher   It doesn't have a proper ending. I never found out who killed Wellington. So the murderer is still At Large.

Siobhan   Not all murders are solved, Christopher. Not all murderers are caught.

Christopher   I don't like the idea that he could be living somewhere nearby and that I might meet him when I go out for a walk at night.

Siobhan   I don't think that's going to happen, Christopher.

Christopher   It could do. Murder is usually committed by a person known to the victim.

Father said I was never to mention Mr Shears' name in our house again and that he was an evil man and maybe that meant he was the person who killed Wellington.

Siobhan   Christopher, I think you should do what your father tells you to do.

Mrs Alexander   What happened to you the other day?

Christopher   Which day?

Mrs Alexander   I came out again and you'd gone. I had to eat all the biscuits myself.

Christopher   I went away.

Mrs Alexander   I gathered that.

Christopher   I thought you might ring the police.

Mrs Alexander   Why on earth would I do that?

Christopher   Because I was poking my nose into other people's business and Father said I shouldn't investigate who killed Wellington. And a policeman gave me a caution and if I get into trouble again it will be a lot worse because of the caution.

Mrs Alexander   You're very shy aren't you, Christopher?

Christopher   I'm not allowed to talk to you.

Mrs Alexander   Don't worry, I'm not going to tell the police and I'm not going to tell your father because there's nothing wrong with having a chat. Having a chat is just being friendly, isn't it?

Christopher   I don't do chatting.

Mrs Alexander   Do you like computers?

Christopher   Yes. I like computers. I have a computer at home in my bedroom.

Mrs Alexander   I know. I can see you sitting at your computer in your bedroom sometimes when I look across the street.

Christopher   And I like maths and looking after Toby. And I also like outer space and I like being on my own.

Mrs Alexander   I bet you're very good at maths, aren't you?

Christopher   I am. I'm going to do A-Level Maths next month. And I'm going to get an A grade.

Mrs Alexander   Really? A-Level Maths?

Christopher   Yes. I don't tell lies.

Mrs Alexander   I apologise. I didn't mean to suggest that you were lying. I just wondered if I heard you correctly. I'm a little deaf sometimes.

Christopher   I remember you told me. I'm the first person to do an A-Level from my school because it's a special school.

Mrs Alexander   Well, I am very impressed. And I hope you do get an A.

Christopher   I will.

Mrs Alexander   And the other thing I know about you is your favourite colour is not yellow.

Christopher   No. And it's not brown either. My favourite colour is red. And metal colour. Do you know Mr Shears?

Mrs Alexander   Not really, no. I mean I knew him well enough to say hello and talk to a little in the street, but I didn't know much about him. I think he worked in a bank. The National Westminster in town.

Christopher   I don't know where that is.

Mrs Alexander   It's by the train station.

Christopher   I don't know where the train station is either because I don't like to go anywhere outside unless I'm on the school bus to school.

Mrs Alexander   Yes, I know how you feel.

Christopher   Father said that he is an evil man. Do you know why he said that? Is Mr Shears an evil man?

Mrs Alexander   Why are you asking me about Mr Shears, Christopher? Is this about Wellington? Perhaps it would be best not to talk about these things, Christopher.

Christopher   Why not?

Mrs Alexander   Because. Because maybe your father is right and you shouldn't go round asking questions about this.

Christopher   Why?

Mrs Alexander   Because obviously he is going to find it quite upsetting.

Christopher   Why is he going to find it quite upsetting?

Mrs Alexander   Because . . . because I think you know why your father doesn't like Mr Shears very much.

Christopher   Did Mr Shears kill Mother?

Mrs Alexander   Kill her?

Christopher   Yes. Did he kill Mother?

Mrs Alexander   No. No. Of course he didn't kill your mother.

Christopher   But did he give her stress so that she died of a heart attack?

Mrs Alexander   I honestly don't know what you're talking about, Christopher.

Christopher   Or did he hurt her so that she had to go into hospital?

Mrs Alexander   Did she have to go into hospital?

Christopher   Yes. And it wasn't very serious at first but she had a heart attack when she was in hospital.

Mrs Alexander   Oh my goodness.

Christopher   And she died.

Mrs Alexander   Oh my goodness. Oh Christopher, I am so, so sorry. I never realised.

Christopher   Why did you say 'I think you know why your father doesn't like Mr Shears very much'?

Mrs Alexander   Oh dear, dear, dear. So you don't know?

Christopher   Don't know what?

Mrs Alexander   Christopher look, I probably shouldn't be telling you this. Perhaps we should take a little walk in the park together. This is not the place to be talking about this kind of thing.

Ed *starts watching their conversation.*

Mrs Alexander   I am going to say something to you and you must promise not to tell your father that I told you this.

Christopher   Why?

Mrs Alexander   I shouldn't have said what I said. And if I don't explain, you'll carry on wondering what I meant. And you might ask your father. And I don't want you to do that because I don't want you to upset him. So I'm going to explain why I said what I said. But before I do that you have to promise not to tell anyone I said this to you.

Christopher   Why?

Mrs Alexander   Christopher, please, just trust me.

Christopher   I promise.

Mrs Alexander   Your mother before she died was very good friends with Mr Shears.

Christopher   I know.

Mrs Alexander   No Christopher, I'm not sure that you do. I mean that they were very good friends. Very, very good friends.

Christopher   Do you mean that they were doing sex?

Mrs Alexander   Yes, Christopher. That is what I mean.

I'm sorry, Christopher. I really didn't mean to say anything that was going to upset you. But I wanted to explain. Why I said what I said. You see I thought you knew. That's why your father thinks Mr Shears is an evil man. And that will be why he doesn't want you going around talking to people about Mr Shears. Because that will bring back bad memories.

Christopher   Was that why Mr Shears left Mrs Shears, because he was doing sex with someone else when he was married to Mrs Shears?

Mrs Alexander   Yes. I expect so. I'm sorry, Christopher. I really am.

Christopher   I think I should go now.

Mrs Alexander   Are you OK, Christopher?

Christopher   I can't be on my own with you because you are a stranger.

Mrs Alexander   I'm not a stranger, Christopher, I'm a friend.

Ed   And what have you been up to, young man?

Christopher   I went to the shop to get some liquorice laces and a Milky Bar.

Ed   You were a long time.

Christopher   I talked to Mrs Alexander's dog outside the shop.

Rhodri   God you do get the third degree, don't you? So how are you doing, captain?

Christopher   I'm doing very well, thank you, Rhodri.

Rhodri   What's 251 times 864?

Christopher   216, 864. Is that right?

Rhodri   I haven't got a bloody clue.

Ed   I'll stick one of these Gobi Aloo Sag things in the oven for you, OK?

Christopher   OK.

Rhodri   With your little bottle of red paint in it, eh Christopher?

Christopher   It's not red paint, it's red food colouring because I don't eat yellow food. If you put red paint into a curry it would be extremely dangerous and it would probably kill you.

Siobhan   Have you told your father about this?

Christopher   No.

Siobhan   Are you going to tell your father about this?

Christopher   No.

Ed *goes to* **Siobhan**.

He looks at her holding the book.

He reaches his hand out for it.

After a short time she passes it to him.

He finds the place she was at.

He begins reading **Christopher***'s book.*

Siobhan   Did it make you sad to find this out?

Christopher   Find what out?

Siobhan   Did it make you sad to find out that your mother and Mr Shears had an affair?

Christopher   No.

Siobhan   Are you telling the truth, Christopher?

Christopher   I always tell the truth. I don't feel sad about it because Mother is dead and because Mr Shears isn't around any more. So I would be feeling sad about something that isn't real and doesn't exist and that would be stupid.

Siobhan   What was your mother like, Christopher?

Do you remember much about her?

Christopher   I remember the 4th of July 2006. I was nine years old. It was a Saturday. We were on holiday in Cornwall. We were on the beach in a place called Polperro. Mother was wearing a pair of shorts made out of denim and a light blue bikini top and she was smoking cigarettes called Consulate, which were mint flavour. And she wasn't swimming. She was sunbathing on a towel, which had red and purple stripes, and she was reading a book by Georgette Heyer called *The Masqueraders*. And then she finished sunbathing and went into the water and she said

Judy   Bloody Nora, it's cold.

Christopher (*simultaneously*)   'Bloody Nora, it's cold.' And she said I should come and swim too, but I didn't like swimming because I don't like taking my clothes off. And she said I should just roll up my trousers and walk into the water a little way. So I did. And Mother said

Judy   Look, it's lovely.

Christopher   And she jumped backwards and disappeared under the water and I thought a shark had eaten her and I screamed. And she stood up out of the water again and came over to where I was standing and held up her right hand and spread out her fingers like a fan.

Judy   Come on, Christopher, touch my hand. Come on now. Stop screaming. Touch my hand. Listen to me, Christopher. You can do it. It's OK, Christopher. It's OK. There aren't any sharks in Cornwall.

Ed   'When we were inside the park Mrs Alexander stopped walking and said "I am going to say something to you and you must promise not to tell your father that I told you this".'

Christopher   And other times she used to say

Judy   If I hadn't married your father I think I'd be living in a little farmhouse in the South of France with someone called Jean. And he'd be, ooh, a local handyman. You know, doing painting and decorating for people, gardening, building fences. And we'd have a veranda with figs growing over it and there would be a field of sunflowers at the bottom of the garden and a little town on the hill in the distance and we'd sit outside in the evening and drink red wine and smoke Gauloise cigarettes and watch the sun go down.

Ed   What is this?

Christopher *looks at* **Ed**.

Christopher   It's a book I'm writing.

Ed   Is this true? Did you speak to Mrs Alexander?

Christopher   Yes.

Ed   Jesus, Christopher, how stupid are you? What the hell did I tell you, Christopher?

Christopher   Not to mention Mr Shears name in the house. And not to go asking Mrs Shears, or anyone, about who killed that bloody dog. And not to go trespassing on other people's gardens. And to stop this bloody ridiculous detective game. Except I haven't done any of those things. I just asked Mrs Alexander about Mr Shears because . . .

Ed   Don't give me that bollocks, you little shit. You knew exactly what you were bloody doing. I've read the book, remember. What else did I say, Christopher?

Christopher   I don't know.

Ed   Come on, you're the memory man. Not to go round sticking your nose into other people's business. And what do you do? You go around sticking your nose into other people's business. You go around raking up the past and sharing it with every Tom, Dick and Harry you bump into. What am I going to do with you, Christopher? What am I going to do with you, Christopher?

Christopher   I was just chatting with Mrs Alexander. I wasn't doing investigating.

Ed   I ask you to do one thing for me, Christopher. One thing.

Christopher   I didn't want to talk to Mrs. Alexander. It was Mrs Alexander who . . .

Ed *grabs* **Christopher***'s arm.*

Christopher *screams.*

Ed *shakes* **Christopher** *hard with both hands.*

Christopher *punches* **Ed** *repeatedly in the face. He cuts his mouth.*

Ed *hits the side of* **Christopher***'s head.*

Christopher *falls unconscious for a few seconds.*

Ed *stands above him. He is still holding the book.*

Ed   I need a drink.

He leaves.

He comes back without the book. He looks at **Christopher** *for a while before he speaks.*

Everybody else on stage watches what he says.

Ed   I'm sorry I hit you.

I didn't mean to.

I love you very much, Christopher. Don't ever forget that. I know I lose my rag occasionally. And I know I shouldn't. But I only do it because I worry about you, because I don't want to see you getting into trouble, because I don't want you to get hurt. Do you understand?

Christopher   Where's my book?

Ed   Christopher, do you understand that I love you?

Ed *holds his right hand up and spreads his fingers out in a fan.*

Christopher *does the same with his left hand.*

They make their fingers and thumbs touch each other.

Christopher   Is it in the dustbin at the front of the house?

Siobhan   Christopher, why have you got a bruise on the side of your face?

Christopher   Father was angry. He grabbed me so I hit him and then we had a fight.

Siobhan   Did he hit you?

Christopher   I don't know. I got very cross. It made my memory go strange.

Siobhan   Did he hit you because he was angry?

Christopher   He didn't hit me. He grabbed me. But he was angry.

Siobhan   Did he grab you hard?

Christopher   Yes.

Siobhan   Christopher, are you frightened of going home?

Christopher   No. Because I need to find my book.

Siobhan   Do you want to talk about it any more?

Christopher   No. Because grabbing is OK if it's on your arm or your shoulder when you are angry, but you can't grab someone's hair or their face. But hitting is not allowed, except if you are already in a fight with someone then it is not so bad.

Siobhan   When I got home from school Father was still at work so I went outside and looked inside the dustbin.

But the book wasn't there.

I wondered if Father had put it into his van and driven to the tip and put it into one of the big bins there but I did not want that to be true because then I would never see it again. One other possibility was that Father had hidden my book somewhere in the house. So I decided to do some detecting and see if I could find it.

I started by looking in the kitchen.

Then I detected in the utility room.

Then I detected in the dining room.

Then I detected in the living room where I found the missing wheel from my Airfix Messerschmitt Bf 109 G-6 model under the sofa.

Then I went upstairs but I didn't do any detecting in my own room because I reasoned that Father wouldn't hide something from me in my own room unless he was being very clever and doing what is called a Double Bluff like in a real murder mystery novel, so I decided to look in my own room only if I couldn't find the book anywhere else.

I detected in the bathroom, but the only place to look was in the airing cupboard and there was nothing in there.

Which meant the only room left to detect in was Father's bedroom.

I started by looking under the bed.

There were seven shoes and a comb with lots of hair in it and a piece of copper pipe and a chocolate biscuit and a magazine called *Fiesta* and a dead bee and a Homer Simpson pattern tie and a wooden spoon, but not my book. Then I looked in the drawers on either side of the dressing table.

But these only contained aspirin and nail clippers and batteries and dental floss and a tampon and tissues and a spare false tooth but my book wasn't there either.

Then I looked in his clothes cupboard. In the bottom of the cupboard was a large plastic toolbox which was full of tools for doing-it-yourself but I could see these without opening the box because it was made of transparent grey plastic. Then I saw that there was another box underneath the toolbox.

So I lifted the toolbox out of the cupboard.

The other box was an old cardboard box that is called a shirt box because people used to buy shirts in them.

Christopher *finds these things including, finally the shirt box.*

Siobhan   And when I opened the shirt box I saw my book was inside it.

Christopher *finds his book.*

Siobhan   Then I heard his van pulling up outside the house and I knew that I had to think fast and be clever.

I heard Father shutting the door of the van.

And that is when I saw the envelope.

It was an envelope addressed to me and it was lying under my book in the shirt box with some other envelopes. I picked it up.

Christopher *finds the envelope.*

Siobhan   It had never been opened.

It said

Judy   Christopher Boone, 36 Randolph Street, Swindon, Wiltshire.

Siobhan   Then I noticed there were lots of envelopes and they were all addressed to me. And this was interesting and confusing.

And then I noticed how the words 'Christopher' and 'Swindon' were written. They were written like this.

Judy   Christopher. Swindon.

Siobhan   I only know three people who do little circles instead of dots over the letter i. And one of them is Siobhan. And one of them was Mr Loxley who used to teach at the school. And one of them was Mother.

Ed   Christopher?

Christopher   Hello.

Ed   So what have you been up to, young man?

Christopher   Today we did Life Skills with Siobhan. Which was Using Money and Public Transport. And I had tomato soup for lunch and three apples. And I practised some maths in the afternoon and we went for a walk in the park with Mrs Peters and collected leaves for making collages.

Ed   Excellent, excellent. What do you fancy for chow tonight?

Christopher   Baked beans and broccoli.

Ed   I think that can be very easily arranged.

I'm just going to put those shelves up in the living room if that's all right with you. I'll make a bit of a racket, I'm afraid, so if you want to watch television we're going to have to shift it upstairs.

Christopher   I'll go and be on my own in my room.

Ed   Good man.

Siobhan   I went up to my room. And when I was in the room I shut the door and took out the envelope. I opened the envelope. Inside there was a letter. And this was what was written in the letter.

Judy   451c Chapter Road, Willesden, London NW2 5NG. 0208 887 8907. Dear Christopher. I'm sorry it's been such a very long time since I wrote my last letter to you. I've been very busy. I've got a new job working as a secretary for a factory that makes things out of steel. You'd like it a lot. The factory is full of huge machines that make the steel and cut it and bend it into whatever shapes they need. Also we've moved into a new flat at last as you can see from the address. It's not as nice as the old one and I don't like Willesden very much, but it's easier for Roger to get to work and he's bought it (he only rented the other one) so we can get our own furniture and paint the walls the colour we want to. You haven't written to me yet, so I know that you are probably still angry with me. I'm sorry, Christopher. But I still love you. I hope you don't stay angry with me for ever. And I'd love it if you were able to write me a letter (but remember to send it to the new address!).

I think about you all the time.

Lots of love,

Your Mum.

Siobhan   I was really confused. Mother had never worked as a secretary for a firm that made things out of steel. And Mother had never lived in London. And Mother had never written a letter to me before.

There was no date on the letter so I couldn't work out when Mother had written the letter and then I looked at the front of the envelope and I saw there was a postmark and there was a date on the postmark which meant that the letter was posted eighteen months after Mother had died.

Ed   What are you doing?

Christopher   I'm reading a letter.

Ed   I've finished the drilling. That David Attenborough nature programme's on telly if you're interested.

Christopher   OK.

Ed *leaves.*

Christopher *watches him go. He looks at the letter. He folds it and puts it back in its envelope and hides it in the box he's sitting on.*

Siobhan   When I started writing my book there was only one mystery to solve. Now there were two. Perhaps the letter was in the wrong envelope and it had been written before Mother had died. Perhaps it wasn't a letter from Mother. Perhaps it was a letter to another person called Christopher from that Christopher's mother. Perhaps someone else had written the letter and pretended to be Mother.

I decided that I would not think about it any more that night because I didn't have enough information and could easily LEAP TO THE WRONG CONCLUSIONS.

He lies down. He curls himself up into a ball.

Night falls. Morning rises.

The next day **Christopher** *comes home from school.*

Ed   You're soaking.

Christopher   Yes.

Ed   Give me your coat, I'll hang it up.

How was school?

Christopher   It was good, thank you.

Joseph Fleming took his trousers off and went to the toilet all over the floor of the changing room and started to eat it, but Mr Davis stopped him.

Ed   Good old Mr Davis eh?

Christopher   Joseph eats everything.

Ed   Does he?

Christopher   He once ate one of the little blocks of blue disinfectant, which hang inside the toilets. And he once ate a £50 note from his mother's wallet. And he eats string and rubber bands and tissues and writing paper and paints and plastic forks. Also he bangs his chin and screams a lot.

Ed   I know how he feels. Christopher –

Christopher   Tyrone said that there was a horse and a pig in the poo so I said he was being stupid, but Siobhan said he wasn't. They were small plastic animals from the library that the staff use to make people tell stories. And Joseph had eaten them.

Ed   Christopher, I've got to go out.

Christopher   Why?

Ed   I've just had a call. There's a lady. Her cellar has flooded. I've got to go out and fix it.

Christopher   Is it an emergency?

Ed   Yes mate.

Christopher   Why can't Rhodri go?

Ed   He's already out on a call.

Christopher   So there are two emergencies.

Ed   That's right, mate.

Christopher   It is raining very heavily.

Ed   It is.

Christopher   The rain looks like white sparks.

Ed   Christopher, if I go out will you be OK?

Christopher   Yes I will because there's no one around because everybody's staying indoors.

Ed   Good. Good. Good. Good lad.

Christopher   I like looking at the rain.

Ed   Terrific.

Christopher   I like it because it makes me think how all the water in the world is connected.

Ed   Does it?

Christopher   This water, this rain has evaporated actually from somewhere like maybe the Gulf of Mexico maybe or Baffin Bay and now it's falling in front of the house and it will drain away into the gutter and flow to a sewage station and then it will be cleaned and then it will go into a river and then it will go back into the ocean again.

Ed   I'll have my mobile with me.

Christopher   Yes.

Ed   So you can call me if there's a problem.

Christopher   Yes.

Ed   Behave yourself, Christopher yeah?

Christopher   Yes.

Ed *remains on stage.*

Siobhan   So I went into his bedroom and opened up the cupboard and lifted the toolbox off the top of the shirt box and opened the shirt box. I counted out the letters. There were forty-three of them. They were all addressed to me in the same handwriting. I took one and opened it. Inside was this letter.

As **Judy** *reads so* **Christopher** *begins to assemble his train set. His building becomes frantic. At times almost balletic.*

Judy   451c Chapter Road, London NW2 5NG. 0208 887 8907. I was looking through some old photos last night, which made me sad. Then I found a photo of you playing with the train set we bought for you a couple of Christmases ago. And that made me happy because it was one of the really good times we had together. Do you remember how you played with it all day and you refused to go to bed at night because you were still playing with it? We told you about train timetables and you made a train timetable and you had a clock and you made the train run on time. And there was a little wooden station, too, and we showed you how people who wanted to go on the train went to the station and bought a ticket and then got on a train? And then we got out a map and we showed you the little lines which were the train lines connecting all the stations. And you played with it for weeks and weeks and weeks and we bought you more trains and you knew where they were all going. I liked remembering that a lot.

Siobhan   Then I opened another envelope. This was the letter that was inside.

Christopher *continues to build a train set. It should be as big as he can possibly make it. He makes it with attention and detail as the letter continues.*

Judy   Dear Christopher. I said that I wanted to explain to you why I went away when I had the time to do it properly. Now I have lots of time. So I'm sitting on the sofa here with this letter and the radio on and I'm going to try and explain.

I was not a very good mother, Christopher. Maybe if things had been different, maybe if you'd been different, I might have been better at it. But that's just the way things turned out.

I'm not like your father. Your father is a much more patient person. He just gets on with things and if things upset him he doesn't let it show.

But that's not the way I am and there's nothing I can do to change it.

Do you remember once when we were shopping in town together? And we went into Bentall's and it was really crowded and we had to get a Christmas present for Grandma? And you were frightened because of all the people in the shop. It was the middle of Christmas shopping when everyone was in town. And I was talking to Mr Land who works on the kitchen floor and went to school with me. And you crouched down on the floor and put your hands over your ears and you were in the way of everyone so I got cross because I don't like shopping at Christmas either, and I told you to behave and I tried to pick you up and move you. But you shouted and you knocked those mixers off the shelf and there was a big crash. And everyone turned round to see what was going on and Mr Land was really nice about it but there were boxes and bits of string and bits of broken bowl on the floor and everyone was staring and I saw that you had wet yourself and I was so cross and I wanted to take you out of the shop but you wouldn't let me touch you and you just lay on the floor and screamed and banged your hands and feet on the floor and the manager came and asked me what the problem was and I was at the end of my tether and I had to pay for two broken mixers and we just had to wait until you stopped screaming. And then I had to walk you all the way home, which took hours because I knew you wouldn't go on the bus again.

And I remember that night I just cried and cried and cried and your father was really nice about it at first and he made you supper and put you to bed and he said these things happen and it would be OK. But I said I couldn't take it any more and eventually he got really cross and he told me I was being stupid and said I should pull myself together and I hit him, which was wrong, but I was so upset.

We had a lot of arguments like that.

Because I often thought I couldn't take it any more. And your father is really patient, but I'm not. I get cross, even though I don't mean to. And by the end we stopped talking to each other very much because we knew it would always end up in an argument. And I felt really lonely.

Siobhan   And that was when I started spending lots of time with Roger.

Judy   And that was when I started spending lots of time with Roger.

Christopher *moves to the middle of the track. He crouches down. He rolls himself into a ball. He starts hitting his hands and his feet and his head against the floor as the letter continues.*

Judy   And I know you might not understand any of this, but I wanted to try to explain so that you knew.

Siobhan   We had a lot in common. And then we realised that we were in love with one ano –

Judy   I said that I couldn't leave you and he was sad about that but he understood that you were really important to me.

Siobhan   And you started to shout and I got cross and I threw the food across the room. Which I know I shouldn't have done.

Judy   You grabbed the chopping board and you threw it and it hit my foot and broke my toes.

Siobhan   And afterwards at home your father and I had a huge argument.

Judy   And I couldn't walk properly for a month, do you remember, and your father had to look after you.

Siobhan   And I remember looking at the two of you and seeing you together and thinking how you were really different with him. Much calmer.

Judy   And it made me so sad because it was like you didn't need me at all.

Siobhan   And I think then I realised you and your father were probably better off if I wasn't living in the house.

Judy   And Roger asked me if I wanted to come with him.

Siobhan   And it broke my heart but eventually I decided it would be better for all of us if I went.

Judy   And so I said yes.

Siobhan   And I meant to say goodbye.

Judy   But when I rang your father he said I couldn't –

He was really angry. He said I couldn't –

Siobhan   He said I couldn't talk to you.

Judy   And I didn't know what to do.

Siobhan   He said I was being selfish and that I was never to set foot inside the house again.

Judy   And so I haven't.

Siobhan   I wonder if you can understand any of this. I know it will be difficult for you.

Judy   I thought what I was doing was the best for all of us. I hope it is.

Siobhan   Christopher, I never meant to hurt you.

Judy   I used to have dreams that everything would get better. Do you remember you used to say that you wanted to be an astronaut? Well I used to have dreams where you were an astronaut and you were on television and I thought that's my son. I wonder what it is that you want to be now. Has it changed? Are you still doing maths? I hope you are.

Have you got the present I sent you? Have you solved it yet? Roger and I saw it in a shop in Camden market and I know you've always liked puzzles.

Siobhan   Roger tried to get the two pieces apart before we wrapped it up and he couldn't do it.

He said that if you managed it you were a genius.

Judy   Loads and loads of love, Mother.

Christopher's *thrashing has exhausted him.*

He has been sick. He lies still for a while, wrapped in a ball.

The box of his mother's letters is next to him.

Ed   Christopher? Christopher?

Christopher *doesn't respond.*

Ed   Christopher, what the hell are you doing? These are. Oh shit. Oh Christ.

Christopher *doesn't move or respond.*

Ed *stops himself from crying.*

Ed   It was an accident.

Christopher *doesn't respond.*

Ed   I don't know what to say . . . I was in such a mess . . . I said she was in hospital. Because I didn't know how to explain, it was so complicated. And once I'd said that . . . I couldn't change it. It just . . . It got out of control.

Christopher *doesn't respond.*

After a time **Ed** *approaches him.*

Very, very gently he touches his shoulder. **Christopher** *doesn't respond.*

Ed   Christopher, we have to get you cleaned up, OK?

Let's sit you up and get your clothes off and get you into bed, OK? I'm going to have to touch you, but it's going to be all right.

Ed *lifts* **Christopher** *on to the side of the bed.* **Christopher** *doesn't resist or fight at all.*

Ed *takes* **Christopher**'s *jumper and shirt off.*

Siobhan *has entered. She has a tube of Smarties.*

Siobhan   Christopher, what do you think is in here?

Christopher   Smarties.

She opens it.

Siobhan   It's not Smarties. It's a pencil. If your Dad came in now, and we asked him what was inside the Smarties tube, what do you think he would say?

Christopher   A pencil.

Ed   Have you had anything to eat this evening?

Can I get you anything to eat, Christopher?

OK. Look. I'm going to go and put your clothes into the washing machine and then I'll come back, OK?

Ed *leaves.* **Christopher** *sits alone and counts.*

Christopher   2, 4, 8, 16, 32, 64, 128, 256, 512, 1024, 2048, 4096, 8192, 16384, 32768, 65536, 131072, 262144, 524288, 1048576, 2097152, 4194304, 8388608, 16777216, 33554432.

Ed   How are you feeling? Can I get you anything?

Look maybe I shouldn't say this, but . . . I want you to know that you can trust me. Life is difficult, you know. It's bloody hard telling the truth all the time. But I want you to know that I'm trying. And perhaps this is not a very good time to say this, and I know you're not going to like it, but . . . You have to know that I am going to tell you the truth from now on. About everything. Because . . . if you don't tell the truth now, then later on it hurts even more. So . . . I killed Wellington, Christopher. Just . . . let me explain. When your mum left . . . Eileen . . . Mrs Shears . . . she was very good to me. She helped me through a very difficult time. And I'm not sure I would have made it without her. Well, you know how she was round here most days. Popping over to see if we were OK. If we needed anything . . . I thought . . . Well . . . Shit, Christopher, I'm trying to keep this simple . . . I thought she might carry on coming over . . . I thought . . . and maybe I was being stupid . . . I thought she might . . . eventually . . . want to move in here. Or that we might move into her house. We . . . we got on really, really well. I thought we were friends. And I guess I thought wrong. We argued, Christopher, and . . . She said some things I'm not going to say to you because they're not nice, but they hurt, but . . . I think she cared more for that bloody dog than for us. And maybe that's not so stupid, looking back. Maybe it's easier living on your own looking after some stupid mutt than sharing your life with other actual human beings. I mean, shit, buddy we're not exactly low maintenance, are we? Anyway, we had this row. Well, quite a few rows to be honest. But after this particularly nasty little blow-out, she chucked me out of the house. And you know what that bloody dog was like. Nice as pie one moment, roll over, tickle its stomach. Sink its teeth into your leg the next. Anyway, we're yelling at each other and it's in the garden. So when she slams the door behind me the bugger's waiting for me. And . . . I know, I know. Maybe if I'd just given it a kick it would probably have backed off. But, shit Christopher, when the red mist comes down. . . Christ, you know what I'm talking about. I mean we're not that different me and you. And it was like everything I'd been bottling up for two years just . . .

I promise you, I never meant for it to turn out like this.

Ed *holds his right hand up for* **Christopher** *to touch.*

Christopher *screams.*

He pushes **Ed** *backwards.*

Ed *stares at* **Christopher**.

Ed   OK. Look. Christopher. I'm sorry. Let's leave it for tonight, OK? I'm going to go downstairs and you get some sleep and we'll talk in the morning. It's going to be all right. Honestly. Trust me.

Ed *leaves.*

Christopher *fields himself into a ball. He groans.*

He starts counting again.

Christopher   2, 4, 8, 16, 32, 64, 128, 256, 512, 1024, 2048, 4096, 8192, 16384, 32768, 32768, 32768, 32768, 32 –

Siobhan   Father had murdered Wellington. That meant he could murder me.

I had to get out of the house.
I had to get out of the house.
I had to get out of the house.
I had to get out of the house.
I had to get out of the house.

I made a decision. I did this by thinking of all the things I could do and deciding whether they were the right decision or not.

Ed   Stay home.

Siobhan   I decided I couldn't stay home any more.

Ed   Christopher, please.

Christopher   No, because I can't live in the house with you any more because it is dangerous.

(*To* **Siobhan**.) I can't go and live with you because you can't look after me when school's closed.

Siobhan   I could try and –

Christopher   No, because you're a teacher.

Siobhan   Yes.

Christopher   Not a friend or a member of my family.

Uncle Terry   You could go and live with your Uncle Terry.

Christopher   You live in Sunderland. I don't know how to get to Sunderland.

Uncle Terry   Get a train. Get the train from Swindon.

Christopher   And you smoke cigarettes. And you stroke my hair.

You're not a friend either.

Mrs Alexander   I think I am a friend.

Christopher   No. And you're not a member of my family.

Mrs Alexander   I do have a dog.

Christopher   Yes but I can't stay overnight in your house or use your toilet because you've used it and you're a stranger.

Mrs Alexander   I'm not really a stranger, Christopher.

Christopher   Yes.

Judy   451c Chapter Road, London NW2 5NG.

451c Chapter Road, London NW2 5NG.

451c Chapter Road, London NW2 5NG.

Christopher *looks at* **Judy**.

Judy   451c Chapter Road.

Christopher   London NW2 5NG.

Light falls.

Part Two

The company is on stage.

Siobhan Christopher, I want to ask you something. Mrs Gascoyne has asked if we would like to do a play this year. She asked me to ask everybody if we'd like to make some kind of performance for the school. Everybody could join in and play a part in it.

Mrs Gascoyne I think it would be a good thing for everybody to join in and play a part in.

Siobhan I was wondering if you'd like to make a play out of your book.

Christopher No.

Siobhan I think it could be really good fun, Christopher.

Mrs Gascoyne I think it could be really good fun.

Christopher No. It's a book and it's for me and not everybody, just for me

Siobhan I know that, Christopher, but I think a lot of people would be interested in what would happen if people took your book and started acting bits out of it.

Christopher No. I don't like acting because it is pretending that something is real when it is not really real at all so it is like a kind of lie.

Siobhan But people like stories, Christopher. Some people find things which are kind of true in things which are made up. You like your Sherlock Holmes stories and you know Sherlock Holmes isn't a real person, don't you?

I would help you if you were worried about that.

Christopher No.

Reverend Peters I think I'd rather like to take the part of a policeman.

Christopher   You're too old to be a policeman.

Ed (*shouting*)   Christopher. Christopher.

Everybody stops what they're doing and watches **Ed**.

Christopher *hides*.

Nobody gives **Ed** *a clue as to where* **Christopher** *is*.

After a while he gives up.

Then **Christopher** *comes out. He is holding Toby in his cage*.

Mrs Alexander   Christopher, what on earth has happened to you?

Christopher   Can you look after Toby for me?

Mrs Alexander   Who's Toby?

Christopher   Toby's my pet rat.

Mrs Alexander   Oh . . . Oh yes. I remember now. You told me.

Christopher   He eats special pellets and you can buy them from a pet shop. And he needs new water in his bottle every day, too.

Mrs Alexander   Why do you need somebody to look after Toby, Christopher?

Christopher   I'm going to London.

Mrs Alexander   How long are you going for?

Christopher   Until I go to university.

Mrs Alexander   Right. Are you and your father moving house?

Christopher   No.

Mrs Alexander   So, why are you going to London?

Christopher   I'm going to live with Mother.

Mrs Alexander   I thought you told me your mother was dead.

Christopher   I thought she was dead but she was still alive. And Father lied to me. And also he killed Wellington and so that means that he could kill me.

Mrs Alexander   Is your mother here?

Christopher   No. Mother is in London. She lives at 451c Chapter Road, London NW2 5NG.

Mrs Alexander   So you're going to London on your own?

Christopher   I think I am going to do that, yes.

Mrs Alexander   Look, Christopher, why don't you come inside and sit down and we can talk about this.

Christopher   No. I can't come inside. Will you look after Toby for me?

Mrs Alexander   I really don't think that would be a good idea, Christopher. Where's your father at the moment, Christopher?

Christopher   I don't know.

Mrs Alexander   Well perhaps we should try and give him a ring and see if we can get in touch with him. I'm sure he's worried about you. And I'm sure that there's been a dreadful misunderstanding.

Christopher *leaves.*

He goes back to his house.

He sees his dad's wallet on the floor. He stares at it, frozen in his tracks.

He approaches the wallet.

He opens the wallet.

He takes out the card from his dad's wallet. He puts it in his pocket.

Christopher   3558. 3558. 3558. 3558. 3558.

He leaves the house.

The company dismantle the house.

They make Swindon town centre.

Christopher   Where can I buy a map?

Lady in Street   Pardon?

Christopher   Where can I buy a map?

Lady in Street   A map of where?

Christopher   A map of here.

Lady in Street   I don't know, where do you want to get to?

Christopher   I'm going to the train station.

Lady in Street   You don't need a map to get to the train station.

Christopher   I do because I don't know where the train station is.

Lady in Street   You can see it from here.

Christopher   No I can't. And also I need to know where there is a cash machine.

Lady in Street   There. That building. Says 'Signal Point' on the top. There's a British Rail sign on the other end. The station's at the bottom of that.

Christopher   Do you mean the stripy building with the horizontal windows that you can see poking out over these houses?

Lady in Street   That's the one.

Christopher   How do I get to that building?

Lady in Street   Gordon Bennett.

Christopher   I knew that the train station was somewhere near. And if something is nearby you can find it by moving in a spiral, walking clockwise and taking every right turn until you come back to a road you've already walked on, then taking the next left, then taking every right turn and so on.

And that was how I found the station.

Voice One   Customers seeking access to the car park please use assistance phone opposite, right of the ticket office.

Voice Two   Warning CCTV in operation.

Voice Three   Great Western.

Voice Five   Cold beers and lagers.

Voice Two   CAUTION WET FLOOR.

Voice Four   Your 50p will keep a premature baby alive for 1.8 seconds.

Voice Three   Transforming travel.

Voice Five   Refreshingly Different.

Voice One   It's Delicious, it's creamy and it's only £1.30. Hot Choc Deluxe.

Voice Two   0870 777 7676.

Voice Four   The Lemon Tree.

Voice One   No Smoking.

Voice Two   Fine teas.

Voice Five   Automatic Fire Door Keep Clear.

Voice Two   Air Conditioned.

Voice Three   Reserved Parking.

Voice Four   Open As Usual This Way.

Voice Three   No Smoking.

Voice Five   No alcohol.

Voice Three   Dogs must be carried.

Voice One   RVP.

Voice Three   Dogs must be carried.

Voice One   LFB.

Voice Four   A Perfect Blend.

Voice Two   Royal Mail.

Voice Four   Mon–Fri 7 am – 7 pm.

Voice Three   Dogs must be carried at all times.

Voice Five   Special Lunch Offers.

Voice One   Parking Subject to the Railway Bylaws Section 219 of the Transport Act 2000.

Voice Three   Please stand on the right.

Voice Four   Superb Coffee.

Voice Two   Step-free Access.

Voice Five   Take Extra Care with Children.

Voice Four   Superb Coffee.

Voice Three   Cash Dispensers.

Voice Four   Superb Coffee.

Voice Three   Dogs must be carried at all times.

Station Policeman   Are you all right, young man?

Christopher   You're too old.

Station Policeman   Are you all right, young man?

Christopher   You're too old to play a policeman.

Station Policeman   Are you all right, young man?

Christopher   No.

Station Policeman   You're looking a bit worse for wear. The lady at the café says that when she tried talking to you, you were in a complete trance. What's your name?

Christopher   Christopher Boone.

Station Policeman   Where do you live?

Christopher   36 Randolph Street.

Station Policeman   What are you doing here?

Christopher   I needed to sit down and be quiet and think.

Station Policeman   OK let's keep it simple. What are you doing at the railway station?

Christopher   I'm going to see Mother.

Station Policeman   Mother?

Christopher   Yes, Mother.

Station Policeman   When's your train?

Christopher   I don't know. She lives in London. I don't know when there's a train to London.

Station Policeman   So, you don't live with your mother?

Christopher   No. But I'm going to.

Station Policeman   So where does your mother live?

Christopher   In London.

Station Policeman   Yes, but where in London?

Christopher   451c Chapter Road, London NW2 5NG.

Station Policeman   Jesus. What is that?

Christopher   That's my pet rat, Toby.

Station Policeman   A pet rat?

Christopher   Yes, a pet rat. He's very clean and he hasn't got bubonic plague.

Station Policeman   Well, that's reassuring.

Christopher   Yes.

Station Policeman   Have you got a ticket?

Christopher   No.

Station Policeman   So how precisely were you going to get to London then?

Christopher   I have a cashpoint card.

Station Policeman   Is this your card?

Christopher   No, it's Father's.

Station Policeman   Father's.

Christopher   Yes, Father's.

Station Policeman   OK.

Christopher   He told me the number. It's 3558.

Station Policeman   Why don't you and I take a stroll to the cash machine, eh?

Christopher   You mustn't touch me.

Station Policeman   Why would I want to touch you?

Christopher   I don't know.

Station Policeman   Well, neither do I.

Christopher   Because I got a caution for hitting a policeman but I didn't mean to hurt him and if I do it again I'll get into even bigger trouble.

Voice One   Please insert your card.

Station Policeman   You're serious, aren't you?

Christopher   Yes.

Voice One   Enter your personal number.

Station Policeman   You lead the way.

Christopher   Where?

Station Policeman   Back by the ticket office.

Voice One   Please enter amount. Ten pounds. Twenty pounds. Fifty pounds. One hundred pounds.

Christopher   How much does it cost to get a ticket to London?

Station Policeman   About twenty quid.

Voice One   Please wait. Your transaction is being processed.

Christopher   Is that pounds?

Station Policeman   Christ alive. Yep. It's twenty pounds.

Voice One   Please take your card and wait for your cash.

Beat.

Station Policeman   Well I guess I shouldn't keep you chatting any longer.

Christopher   Where do I get a ticket for the train from?

Station Policeman   You are a prize specimen, aren't you?

Christopher   Where do I get a ticket for the train from?

Station Policeman   In there. Now are you sure you know what you're doing?

Christopher   Yes. I'm going to London to live with my mother.

Station Policeman   Has your mother got a telephone number?

Christopher   Yes.

Station Policeman   And can you tell me what it is?

Christopher   Yes. It's 020 887 8907.

Station Policeman   And you'll ring her if you get into any trouble, OK?

Christopher   I want to go to London.

Man behind Counter   If you don't mind.

Christopher   I want to go to London.

Man behind Counter   Single or return?

Christopher   What does 'single or return' mean?

Man behind Counter   Do you want to go one way or do you want to come back?

Christopher   I want to stay there when I get there.

Man behind Counter   For how long?

Christopher   Until I go to university.

Man behind Counter   Single then. That'll be £17.

Christopher   When is the train to London?

Man behind Counter   Platform One, five minutes.

Christopher   Where is Platform One?

Man behind Counter   Through the underpass and up the stairs. You'll see the signs.

Siobhan   Underpass means tunnel, Christopher.

Somebody bumps into **Christopher**. *He barks at them like a dog.*

Siobhan   In your head imagine a big red line across the floor. It starts at your feet and goes through the tunnel. And walk along the line. And count the rhythm in your head because that helps, doesn't it? Like when you're doing music or when you're doing drumming. Left, right, left, right, left, right.

Christopher   Left, right, left, right, left, right.

Siobhan   See the sign saying Platform One. See the glass door. Go through the glass door, Christopher.

Somebody bumps into **Christopher** *again. Again he barks like a dog.*

Whole Company   Watch where the hell you're going.

Siobhan   Watch that man. There. See where he presses the button. And the doors slide open.

You do that.

Press the button.

Step through the doors.

Christopher   Is this the train to London?

Station Policeman   Christopher. Caught you. Just in time. We've got your father at the police station. He's looking for you.

Christopher   I know.

Station Policeman   So why are you going to London?

Christopher   Because I'm going to live with Mother.

Station Policeman   Well, I think your father might have something to say about that.

Christopher *tries to run. The* **Policeman** *grabs him.* **Christopher** *screams. The* **Policeman** *lets go.*

Station Policeman   OK, let's not get over-excited here. I'm going to take you back to the police station and you and me and your dad can sit down and have a little chat about who's going where.

Christopher   Have you arrested Father?

Station Policeman   Arrested him? What for?

Christopher   He killed a dog. With a garden fork. The dog was called Wellington.

Station Policeman   Well, we can talk about that as well. Right now, young man, I think you've done enough adventuring for one day.

The **Policeman** *reaches out to touch him. He screams.*

Now listen, you little monkey. You can either do what I say, or I'm going to have to make . . .

The train begins to move.

Bollocks.

Christopher   Why are you swearing? Have we started? Has the train started?

Station Policeman   Don't move.

Rob? Yeah it's Nigel. I'm stuck here on the bloody train. Yeah. Don't even. . . Look. It stops at Didcot Parkway. So if you can get someone to meet me with a car. . . Cheers. Tell his old man we've got him but it's going to take a while, OK? Great. Let's get ourselves a seat. Park yourself. You are a bloody handful you are. Jeez.

The company rebuild and extend and develop the interior of the train. Including the luggage rack.

Christopher   I see everything. Most other people are lazy. They never look at everything. They do what is called glancing, which is the same word for bumping off something and carrying on in almost the same direction. And the information in their head is really simple. For example, if they are on a train looking out of a window at the countryside it might be

Voice One   1. I am sitting on a train looking out at a field that is full of grass.

Voice Two   2. There are some cows in the field.

Voice Three   3. It is sunny with a few clouds.

Voice Four   4. There are some flowers in the grass.

Voice Five   5. There is a village in the distance.

Voice One   6. There is a fence at the edge of the field and it has a gate in.

Christopher   And then they would stop noticing anything because they would be thinking something else like

Voice Two   Oh it is very beautiful here.

Christopher   Or

Voice One   I'm worried that I might have left the gas cooker on.

Christopher   Or

Voice Four   I wonder if Julie has given birth yet.

Christopher   But if I am standing looking out of the window of a train on to the countryside I notice everything. Like

As **Christopher** *talks he raps out a nervous rhythm with his hand.*

1. There are nineteen cows in the field. Fifteen of which are black and white and four of which are brown and white.

2. There is a village in the distance, which has thirty-one visible houses and a church with a square tower and not a spire.

3. There are ridges in the field which means that in medieval times it was called a ridge and furrow field and people who lived in the village would have a ridge each to do farming on.

4. There is an old plastic bag from Asda in the hedge and a squashed Coca Cola can with a snail on, and a long piece of orange string.

5. The north-east corner of the field is highest and the south-west corner is lowest.

6. I can see three different types of grass and two colours of flowers in the grass.

7. The cows are mostly facing uphill,

And there were thirty-one more things in this list of things.

Station Policeman   Oh Christ, you've wet yourself. For God's sake, go to the bloody toilet, will you?

Christopher   But I'm on a train.

Station Policeman   They do have toilets on trains, you know.

Christopher   Where is the toilet on the train?

Station Policeman   Through those doors there. But I'll be keeping an eye on you, you understand?

Christopher   No.

Station Policeman   Just go to the bloody toilet.

Christopher *stands.*

He walks down the corridor of the train. Shaking, closing his eyes, he pisses.

He tries to wash his hand but can't because there is no running water.

He spits on his hands to wash them. He rubs them dry with toilet paper.

Shaking he leaves the toilet.

He goes to the luggage rack.

He moves two bags.

He climbs on to the shelf.

He hides himself behind the suitcases.

He starts listing prime numbers to himself.

As he continues to count the **Policeman** *notices he's gone. The counting continues under the following exchanges.*

Christopher   2, 3, 5, 7, 11, 13, 17, 19, 23, 29, 31, 37, 41, 43, 47, 53, 59, 61, 67, 71, 73, 79, 83, 89, 97, 101, 103, 107, 109, 113, 127, 131, 137, 139, 149, 151, 157, 163, 167, 173, 179, 181, 191, 193, 197, 199, 211, 223, 227, 229, 233, 239, 241, 251, 257, 263, 269, 271, 277, 281.

Station Policeman   Christopher? Christopher? Bloody hell.

He leaves. **Christopher** *stays where he is. Still counting. A woman approaches him to take her bag.*

Woman on Train   You scared the living daylights out of me. I think someone's out there on the platform looking for you.

Christopher   I know.

Woman on Train   Well. It's your look-out.

She takes her bag. She leaves. **Christopher** *stays hidden behind the smaller pile of bags. Still counting. A* **Posh Man** *approaches. He takes his bag.*

Posh Man   Have you touched my bag?

Christopher   Yes.

He leaves. **Christopher** *stays hidden behind the still smaller pile of bags. Still counting. Two* **Drunk Men** *approach to take their bags.*

Drunk One   Come and look at this, Barry. They've got like, a train elf.

Drunk Two   Well, we have both been drinking.

Drunk One   Perhaps we should feed him some nuts.

Drunk Two   You're the one who's bloody nuts.

Drunk One   Come on, shift it, you daft bugger. I need more beers before I sober up.

Christopher *is revealed now. He stops counting. He lies still for a while. Then very tentatively he gets down.*

He looks around. For the first time he is alone on stage.

Christopher   I waited for nine more minutes but nobody else came past and the train was really quiet. And I didn't move again. So I realised that the train had stopped. And I knew that the last stop on the train was London.

I heard the sound of feet and it was a policeman.

The **Station Policeman** *enters and explores the back of the stage.*

Christopher   Not the one who was on the train before.

The **Station Policeman** *looks at* **Christopher**. *Exits, disappointed. Is replaced by a* **London Transport Policeman**.

Christopher   And I could see him through the door, in the next carriage, and he was looking under the seats. I decided I didn't like policemen so much any more. So I got off the train.

Christopher *kneels down.*

He rests his head on the ground.

He groans.

Siobhan *comes back on to the stage.* **Christopher** *notices her. He stops groaning.*

The two look at one another for a while.

Siobhan   Left right left right left right. Left right left right left right. Left right left right left right.

He smiles at her. He joins in with her. Eventually he carries on without her.

Christopher   Left right left right left right left right left right left right left right left right left right left right.

A **Ticket Collector** *stops him.*

Ticket Collector   I think someone's looking for you, sonny.

Christopher   Who's looking for me?

Ticket Collector   A policeman.

Christopher   I know.

Ticket Collector   Oh right. You wait here, and I'll go and tell them.

The **Ticket Collector** *walks off.* **Christopher** *carries on.*

As he walks he counts left and right.

Christopher   Left, right, left, right, left, right.

Voice One   Sweet Pastries.

Voice Two   Heathrow Airport Check-In Here.

Voice One   Bagel factory.

Voice Five   Eat.

Voice Three   Excellence and taste.

Voice Four   Yo! Sushi.

Voice One   Stationlink.

Voice Two   Buses.

Voice Five   WH Smith.

Voice Four   Mezzanine.

Voice One   Heathrow Express.

Voice Two   Clinique.

Voice Three   First-Class Lounge.

Voice Four   Fullers.

Voice Five   EasyCar.co.

Voice Two   The Mad Bishop.

Voice Three   And Bear Public House.

Voice Four   Fuller's London Pride.

Voice One   Dixons.

Voice Two   Our Price.

Voice Three   Paddington Bear at Paddington Station.

Voice Five   Tickets.

Voice One   Taxis.

Voice Two   First Aid.

Voice Four   Eastbourne Terrace.

Voice Two   Way Out.

Voice One   Praed Street.

Voice Five   The Lawn.

Voice Three   Q Here Please.

Voice Four   Upper Crust.

Voice One   Sainsbury's.

Voice Five   Local information.

Voice Three   Great Western First.

Voice One   Position Closed.

Voice Two   Closed.

Voice Four   Position Closed.

Voice Three   Sock Shop.

Voice Four   Fast Ticket Point.

Voice Five   Millie's Cookies.

Voice One   Coffee.

Voice Two   Fergie to Stay at Manchester United.

Voice Three   Freshly Baked Cookies and Muffins.

Voice Two   Cold Drinks.

Voice Four   Penalty Fares.

Voice One   Warning.

Voice Three   Savoury Pastries.

Voice Four   Platform 14.

Voice Five   Burger King.

Voice Two   Fresh Filled.

Voice Three   The Reef Café Bar.

Voice Four   Business Travel.

Voice One   Special Edition.

Voice Two   Top 75 Albums.

Voice Five   *Evening Standard.*

As the chorus becomes more cacophonous **Christopher** *finds it more difficult to continue to walk.*

He stops. Rests his head against a box. Puts his hands over his ears.

A **Station Guard** *approaches him.*

Station Guard   You look lost.

Christopher *pulls out his Swiss Army knife.*

The **Guard** *backs away.*

Station Guard   Whoa, whoa, whoa, whoa.

Christopher *carries on.*

Christopher   Left right left right left right left right.

He makes his hand into a telescope to limit his field of vision.

He approaches an information counter.

Is this London?

Is this London?

Information   Sure is, honey.

Christopher   Is this London?

Information   Indeed it is.

Christopher   How do I get to 451c Chapter Road, London NW2 5NG?

Information   Where is that?

Christopher   It's 451c Chapter Road, London, NW2 5NG.
And sometimes you can write it 451c Chapter Road,
Willesden, London NW2 5NG.

Information   Take the tube to Willesden Junction. Or
Willesden Green. Got to be near there somewhere.

Christopher   What sort of tube?

Information   Are you for real? Over there. See that big
staircase with the escalators? See the sign? Says
Underground. Take the Bakerloo Line to Willesden
Junction or the Jubilee to Willesden Green. You OK, honey?

Ed   Don't do this, Christopher.

Christopher   Get away from me.

Ed   Christopher, you won't be able to.

Christopher   I'm doing really well.

Ed   Where's your red line gone? See? It's disappearing,
isn't it?

Where's your Swiss Army knife. Have you lost it?

Christopher   It's in my pocket.

Ed   Where?

Christopher   Here.

Ed   How the hell are you going to find the Jubilee Line?
You don't even know what an escalator is, do you?

Christopher   It's a moving staircase. You step on to it. It
carries you down. It's funny. Look.

Ed   Stop laughing. Everybody's looking at you.

Christopher   It's like something out of science fiction.

Ed   I'm worried about you.

Christopher   You're lying. You killed Wellington.

Ed   Where are you going?

Christopher   To watch the people. It's easy, look. You go to the black machine. You look at where you want to go. You find the price. You put your money in.

Ed   You haven't got any money.

Christopher   I have. I stole your card.

Ed   You little shit.

Christopher   You press Ticket Type. You press Adult Single. £2.20. You Insert £2.20. You Take Ticket and Change. You go up to the grey gate. You put your ticket in the slot. It comes out of the other side.

Customer   Get a move on.

Ed   There's no Jubilee Line. How are you going to get on the Jubilee Line to Willesden Green? You're in the wrong place.

Christopher   There's a Bakerloo Line. Look. I can go to Willesden Junction.

Ed   Come back home.

Christopher   I can't.

Ed   You can.

Christopher   You told a lie. You killed Wellington. Swindon's not my home any more. My home is 451c Chapter Road, London NW2 5NG.

Ed *looks at him for a while.*

Ed   Go to the left.

Christopher   I know.

Ed   The train will be very noisy.

Christopher   I know.

Ed   It'll really scare you.

Christopher   I know.

Ed   Try not to let it. Watch what the people do. Watch how they get on and off.

Christopher   Yes.

The company stand with **Christopher** *on the platform.*

Ed   Count the trains. Figure it out. Get the rhythm right.

Train coming. Train stopped. Train going. Silence. Train coming. Train stopped. Train going. Silence.

Christopher   Train coming. Train stopped. Train going. Silence. Train coming. Train stopped. Train going. Silence.

Train coming. Train stopped. Train going. Silence.

Train coming. Train stopped. Train going. Silence.

Train coming. Train stopped. Train going. Silence.

Christopher *goes into his pocket. He can't find Toby.*

Christopher   Toby?

He looks more. He can't find him. He panics. He stands up.

Toby? Where are you?

He explores the stage. He calls for Toby. He stays calm.

Toby? Toby? Toby. What are you doing down there?

He climbs down on to the tracks to rescue Toby.

Man with Socks   Jesus. What are you doing?

Christopher   My rat is on here.

Man with Socks   Get out of there, for Christ's sake.

Christopher   Toby . . . Toby . . . Toby . . .

Man with Socks   Oh Christ. Oh Christ.

The **Man** *pulls* **Christopher** *off the tracks.* **Christopher** *screams for being touched. He calms. He puts Toby back in his pocket.*

Man with Socks   What the hell do you think you were playing at?

Christopher   I was finding Toby. He's my pet rat.

Man with Socks   Bleeding Nora.

Punk Girl   Is he OK?

Man with Socks   Him? Thanks a bundle. Jesus Christ. A pet rat. Oh shit. My train. Bollocks.

Punk Girl   Are you OK?

She touches his arm. He screams.

OK. OK. OK. Is there anything I can do to help you?

Christopher   Stand further away. I've got a Swiss Army knife and it has a saw blade and it could cut someone's finger off.

Punk Girl   OK buddy. I'm going to take that as a no.

Punk Girl *and* **Man with Socks** *leave.* **Christopher** *counts the trains again.*

Christopher   Train coming. Train stopped. Train going. Silence.

Train coming. Train stopped. Train going. Silence.

Train coming. Train stopped. Train going. Silence.

Is this train going to Willesden Junction?

Voice One   There are 53,963 holiday cottages in Scandanavia and Germany.

Voice Two   VITABIOTICS.

Christopher   Is this train going to Willesden Junction?

Voice Three   3435.

Voice Five   Penalty £10 if you fail to show a valid ticket for your entire journey.

Voice Four   Discover Gold, Then Bronze.

Christopher   Is this train going to Willesden Junction?

Voice One   TVIC.

Voice Three   EPBIC.

Voice Five   Obstructing the doors can be dangerous.

Voice Two   BRV.

Voice Three   Con. IC.

Christopher   Is this train going to Willesden Junction?

Voice Four   TALK TO THE WORLD.

Voice One   Warwick Avenue.

Maida Vale.

Kilburn Park.

Queen's Park.

Kensal Green.

Willesden Junction.

Christopher   Where is 451c Chapter Road, London NW2 5NG?

*A **Shopkeeper** shows him an A–Z of London.*

Shopkeeper   A–Z of London. Two ninety-five. Are you going to buy it or not?

Christopher   I don't know.

Shopkeeper   Well you can get your dirty fingers off it if you don't mind.

Christopher   Where is 451c Chapter Road, London NW2 5NG?

Shopkeeper   You can either buy the *A–Z* or you can hop it. I'm not a walking encyclopaedia.

Christopher   Is that the *A–Z*?

Shopkeeper   No, it's a sodding crocodile.

Christopher   Is that the *A–Z*?

Shopkeeper   Yes, it's the *A–Z*?

Christopher   Can I buy it?

Shopkeeper   Two pounds ninety-five, but you're giving me the money first. I'm not having you scarpering.

Christopher *examines the* A–Z. *He opens it. He looks for Chapter Road.*

A **Man on a Phone** *approaches him.*

Man on Phone   Big cheese. Oh yes. The nurses. Never. Bloody liar. Total. Bloody liar.

The **Man** *leaves.*

Christopher *closes the map. He stands up. He looks to the audience. He talks. His voice quietens the more he talks. And as he talks he squats. And then sits. And then huddles into a ball.*

Christopher   Left. Right. Left. Right. Left. Right.

Left.
Right.
Left.
Right.
Left.
Right.
Left.

Christopher *sits silently, huddled for a while.*

Judy *and* **Roger** *enter.*

Judy   I don't care whether you thought it was funny or not.

Roger   Judy look, I'm sorry, OK.

Judy   Well perhaps you should have thought about that before you made me look like a complete idiot.

Christopher *stands up.* **Judy** *sees him.*

The two look at one another.

Christopher   You weren't in so I waited for you.

Judy   Christopher.

Christopher   What?

Judy   Christopher.

She goes to hug him. He pushes her away so hard that he falls over.

Roger   What the hell is going on?

Judy   I'm so sorry, Christopher. I forgot.

Judy *spreads her fingers.* **Christopher** *spreads his to touch hands with her.*

Roger   I suppose this means Ed's here.

Christopher *shows Toby to* **Roger**. **Roger** *recoils.*

Christopher   He's hungry. Have you got any food I can give him and some water.

Judy   Where's your father, Christopher?

Christopher   I think he's in Swindon.

Roger   Thank God for that.

Judy   But how did you get here?

Christopher   I came on the train.

Judy   Oh my God, Christopher. I didn't . . . I didn't think I'd ever . . . Why are you here on your own?

Christopher, you're soaking. Roger, don't just stand there.

Roger   Are you going to come in or are you going to stay out here all night?

Christopher   I'm going to live with you because Father killed Wellington with a garden fork and I'm frightened of him.

Roger   Jumping Jack Christ.

Judy   Roger, please. Come on. Christopher, let's go inside and get you dried off.

Go on or you'll catch your death.

Christopher *doesn't move.*

Judy   You follow Roger.

Christopher *doesn't move.*

Are you OK, Christopher?

Christopher   I'm very tired.

Judy   I know, love. Will you let me help you get your clothes off? I can get you a clean T-shirt. And some runners.

You could get yourself into bed.

She changes him.

He wears one of her old T-shirts.

You're very brave.

Christopher   Yes.

Judy   You never wrote to me.

Christopher   I know.

Judy   Why didn't you write to me, Christopher? I wrote you all those letters. I kept thinking something dreadful had happened or you'd moved away and I'd never find out where you were.

Christopher   Father said you were dead.

Judy   What?

Christopher   He said you went into hospital because you had something wrong with your heart. And then you had a heart attack and died.

Judy   Oh my God.

Judy *starts to howl.*

Christopher   Why are you doing that?

Judy   Oh Christopher, I'm so sorry.

Christopher   It's not your fault.

Judy   Bastard. The Bastard.

Christopher, let me hold your hand. Just for once. Just for me. Will you? I won't hold it hard.

Christopher   I don't like people holding my hand.

Judy   No. OK. That's OK.

London Policeman   I need to speak to him.

Judy   He's been through enough today already.

London Policeman   I know. But I still need to speak to him.

Christopher Boone. Please can you open the door.

Roger   Come on, Christopher.

Judy   Christopher love. It's all right. Just open the door, will you, sweetheart?

Christopher   Is he going to take me away?

Judy   No, Christopher, he isn't.

Christopher   Will you let him take me away?

Judy   No. I won't.

Christopher   Do you promise?

Judy   Yes. I promise.

London Policeman   Your father says you've run away. Is that right?

Christopher   Yes.

London Policeman   Is this your mother?

Christopher   Yes.

London Policeman   Why did you run away?

Christopher   Because Father killed Wellington who is a dog and so that meant that he could kill me.

London Policeman   So I've been told. Do you want to go back to Swindon to your father or do you want to stay here?

Christopher   I want to stay here.

London Policeman   And how do you feel about that?

Christopher   I want to stay here.

London Policeman   Hang on, I'm asking your mother.

Judy   He told Christopher I was dead.

London Policeman   OK. Let's. . . let's not get into an argument about who said what here. I just want to know whether . . .

Judy   Of course he can stay.

London Policeman   Well, I think that probably settles it as far as I'm concerned.

Christopher   Are you going to take me back to Swindon?

London Policeman   No.

If your husband turns up and causes any trouble, just give us a ring. Otherwise you're going to have to sort this out amongst yourselves.

Ed   I'm talking to her whether you like it or not.

Judy   Roger. Don't. Just . . .

Roger   I'm not going to be spoken to like that in my own home.

Ed   I'll talk to you how I damn well like.

Judy   You have no right to be here.

Ed   He's my son in case you've forgotten.

Judy   What in God's name did you think you were playing at saying those things to him?

Ed   You were the one that bloody left.

Judy   So, you decided to just wipe me out of his life altogether?

Roger   Now let's just all calm down here, shall we?

Ed   Well, isn't that what you wanted?

Judy   I wrote to him every week.

Ed   What is the bloody use is writing to him?

Roger   Whoa. Whoa. Whoa.

Ed   I cooked his meals. I cleaned his clothes. I looked after him every weekend. I looked after him when he was ill. I took him to the doctor. I worried myself sick every time he wandered off somewhere at night. I went to school every time he got into a fight. And you? What? You wrote him some sodding letters.

Christopher *gets up out of the sleeping bag.*

Judy   So you thought it was OK to tell him his mother was dead?

Roger   Now is not the time.

Christopher *finds his Swiss Army knife.*

Ed   I'm going to see him. And if you try to stop me . . .

Ed *gets into* **Christopher***'s room.* **Christopher** *points his knife at him.*

Judy *comes in.*

Judy   It's OK, Christopher, I won't let him do anything. You're all right.

Ed   Christopher?

Ed *squats down, completely exhausted.*

Christopher *still points the knife at him.*

Ed   Christopher I'm really, really sorry. About – About – About the letters. I never meant . . . I promise I will never do anything like that again.

Ed *spreads his fingers and tries to get* **Christopher** *to touch him.* **Christopher** *ignores him. He still holds his knife out. He groans.*

Ed   Shit. Christopher, please.

London Policeman   Mr Boone.

Ed   What are you doing here? Did you call him?

London Policeman   Mr Boone, come on mate.

Ed   Don't bleeding mate me. This is my son.

London Policeman   I know. This can all be sorted out. Just come with me. Please.

Judy   I think you should go now. I think he's frightened.

Ed   I'll be back.

Christopher. I'll be back. I promise you, Christopher. I promise you, lad.

Christopher *groans.*

London Policeman *watches* **Ed** *leave.*

Roger *watches them both leave.*

Judy *and* **Christopher** *are left alone together.*

Judy   You go back to sleep now. Everything is going to be all right. I promise.

They leave **Christopher** *in his room. He lies down. He settles.*

Immediately he has settled it is the next morning. **Roger** *and* **Judy** *give* **Christopher** *breakfast. He is overwhelmed by them.*

Roger   OK. He can stay for a few days.

Voice Three   A plate of tomatoes.

Roger *gives him a plate of tomatoes.*

Judy   He can stay as long as he needs to stay.

Voice Six   Some egg whites.

Judy *gives him some egg whites.*

Roger   This flat is hardly big enough for two people, let alone three.

Voice Four   A tin of beans.

Roger *gives him a tin of beans.*

Judy   He can understand what you're saying, you know?

Voice Five   Tomato ketchup.

Judy *gives him tomato ketchup.*

Roger   What's he going to do? There's no school for him to go to. We've both got jobs. It's bloody ridiculous.

Voice One   A strawberry milkshake.

Roger *gives him a strawberry milkshake.*

Judy   Roger. That's enough. You can stay as long as you want to stay.

Christopher   It was Mother who gave me the milkshake.

They look at him.

It was Mother who gave me the milkshake, not you.

Judy *picks the milkshake up.*

Christopher   You need to shout more loudly at him. Like you're really angry with him not just being nice.

Judy *looks at him. Nods.*

Judy   OK.

She puts the milkshake down. She's much angrier.

Roger. That's enough. You can stay as long as you want to stay.

She looks at **Christopher**, *examining his response. Expecting more feedback.*

Christopher   I have to go back to Swindon.

They both look at him.

Judy   Christopher, you've only just got here.

Christopher   I have to go back because I have to sit my Maths A-Level.

Judy   You're doing Maths A-Level?

Christopher   Yes. I'm taking it on Wednesday and Thursday and Friday next week.

Judy   God.

Christopher   The Reverend Peters is going to be the invigilator.

Judy   I mean that's really good.

Christopher   I'm going to get an A grade. And that's why I have to go back to Swindon. Except I can't see Father. So I have to go back to Swindon with you.

Judy   I don't know whether that's going to be possible.

Christopher   But I have to go.

Judy   Let's talk about this some other time, OK?

Christopher   OK. But I have to go to Swindon.

He stands and leaves.

Judy   Christopher. Please.

Christopher   What time is it?

Siobhan   Seven minutes past two in the morning.

Christopher   I can't sleep.

Siobhan   It's because you're scared of Mr Shears. You're being silly.

Christopher   There's nobody about. You can hear traffic.

Christopher *wanders down the street.*

Siobhan   What cars are there?

Christopher   A Fiesta. A Nissan Micra. A Peugeot. A Ford Granada.

Siobhan   What colours are they?

Christopher   I can't tell. I can only see orange and black. And mixtures of orange and black.

Siobhan   Look at the things people have in their front garden.

Christopher   Oh yes. Is that an elf?

Siobhan   It's a gnome. And a teddy bear. And a little pond, look.

Christopher   And a cooker.

I like looking up at the sky.

Siobhan   Me too.

Christopher   When you look at the sky at night you know you are looking at stars, which are hundreds and thousands of light years away from you. And some of the stars don't exist any more because their light has taken so long to get to us that they are already dead, or they have exploded and collapsed into red dwarfs. And that makes you seem very small, and if you have difficult things in your life it is nice to think that they are what is called negligible which means they are so small you don't have to take them into account when you are calculating something.

I can't see any stars here.

Siobhan   No.

Christopher   It's because of all the light pollution in London. All the light from the streetlights and car headlights and floodlights and lights in the buildings reflect off tiny particles in the atmosphere and they get in the way of light from the stars.

Two of the company approach. They talk in Ukrainian.

Ukrainian One   *Ty wedel tovo malchika za mashynoy?* (Can you see that boy hiding behind the car?)

Christopher   Who are they?

Siobhan   Just strangers. Hide down between the skip and the van.

Ukrainian Two   *Da, etot gorod polon grjobanykh sumashedshykh.* (Yes, I swear this city is full of crazy people.)

He hides.

They pass him, chatting in Ukrainian.

Christopher   What language is that?

Siobhan   I think it's Russian. Sshhh.

Christopher   Have they gone? Have they gone? Have they gone? Did they see me?

Judy *starts looking for* **Christopher**.

Judy   Christopher? Christopher?

Christopher *stands up.* **Judy** *stares at him.*

Judy   Jesus Christ. What are you doing out here? I've been looking for you. I thought you'd gone. If you ever do that again, I swear to God, Christopher, I love you, but . . . I don't know what I'll do.

You need to promise me you won't leave the flat on your own again, Christopher. Christopher, do you promise me that?

Christopher   Yes.

Judy   You can't trust people in London.

Christopher   Is it because they're strangers?

Roger   Don't be a bloody fool.

Judy   I'm not being a bloody fool, Roger, they got somebody in. They didn't even call me. They didn't ask me if I wanted to come back. I've been off two days. It's illegal that is.

Roger   It was a temporary job, for Christ's sake.

Christopher   I have to go to Swindon to take my A-Level.

Judy   Christopher, not now.

I'm getting phone calls from your father threatening to take me to court. I'm getting it in the neck from Roger. It's not a good time.

Christopher   But I have to go because it's been arranged and the Reverend Peters is going to invigilate.

Judy   It's only an exam. I can ring the school. We can get it postponed. You can take it some other time.

Christopher   I can't take it another time. It's been arranged. And I've done lots of revision. And Mrs Gascoyne says we could use a room at school.

Judy   Christopher, I am just about holding this together. But I am this close to losing it, all right? So just give me some . . .

She breaks. She cries. She holds her fist to her mouth to try to stop herself.

She leaves the room. She comes back.

Judy   Would you like an iced lolly?

Christopher   Yes I would, please.

Judy   Would you like a strawberry one?

Christopher   Yes I would, please, because that's red. What's it called here?

Judy   It's called Hampstead Heath. I love it. You can see all over London.

Christopher   Where are the planes going to?

Judy   Heathrow, I think.

Christopher, I rang Mrs Gascoyne.

I told her that you're going to take your Maths A-Level next year.

Christopher *screams. He throws his iced lolly away.*

Christopher, please. Calm down. OK. OK, Christopher. Just calm down, love.

Woman on Heath   Is he OK?

Judy   Well, what does it look like to you?

Christopher *screams and screams. He only stops because his chest hurts and he runs out of breath.*

Roger *gives* **Christopher** *a radio and three children's books.*

Roger   Here we are. *100 Number Puzzles*. It's from the library. This one is called *The Origins of the Universe*. And this one is *Nuclear Power*.

Christopher   They're for children.

They're not very good.

I'm not going to read them.

Roger   Well, it's nice to know my contribution is appreciated.

Judy   Christopher, I made you a chart. Because you've got to eat, love. In here is some Complan and it's got strawberry flavouring in it.

Roger   Complan?

Judy   Be quiet, Roger. Christopher, if you drink 200 millilitres then I'm going to put a bronze star on your chart.

Roger   I don't believe this.

Judy   Roger, for God's sake, please. If you drink 400 millilitres you get a silver star.

Roger   Ha!

Judy   And if you drink 600 millilitres you get a gold star.

Roger   A gold star. Well, that's very original I have to say.

Judy   Roger, stop it.

Christopher *picks up the radio. He leaves. He de-tunes it so that it is between two stations. He listens to the white noise. He turns the volume up very high.*

Some time.

Roger *watches him. He opens and drinks four cans of lager. He necks the lager in one go.*

Roger *comes into his room. He is very drunk.*

Roger   You think you're so bloody clever, don't you? Don't you ever, ever think about other people for one second, eh? Well, I bet you're really pleased with yourself now, aren't you?

He grabs at **Christopher**. **Christopher** *rolls himself into a ball to hide.*

Judy *comes into the room. She grabs* **Roger**. *She pulls him away from* **Christopher**.

Christopher *is moaning still in his ball.*

Judy   Christopher, I'm sorry. I'm really, really sorry.

He remains in his ball.

He doesn't stop moaning.

Judy *and* **Roger** *leave.*

Eventually he calms.

Christopher   What time is it?

Judy   It's four o'clock.

Christopher   What are you doing?

Judy   I'm packing some clothes.

Christopher   Where's Mr Shears?

Judy   He's asleep.

Come downstairs. Bring Toby. Get into the car.

Christopher   Into Mr Shears car?

Judy   That's right.

Christopher   Are you stealing the car?

Judy   I'm just borrowing it.

Christopher   Where are we going?

Judy   We're going home.

Christopher   Do you mean home in Swindon?

Judy   Yes.

Christopher   Is Father going to be there?

Judy   Please, Christopher. Don't give me any hassle right now, OK?

Christopher   I don't want to be with Father.

Judy   Just . . . just . . . it's going to be all right, Christopher, OK? It's going to be all right.

Christopher   Are we going back to Swindon so I can do my Maths A-Level?

Judy   What?

Christopher   I'm meant to be doing my Maths A-Level tomorrow.

Judy   We're going back to Swindon because if we stay in London any longer. . . someone was going to get hurt. And I don't necessarily mean you.

Now I need you to be quiet for a while.

Christopher   How long do you need me to be quiet for?

Judy   Jesus. Half an hour, Christopher. I need you to be quiet for half an hour.

Ed   How did you get in here?

Judy   This is my house too, in case you've forgotten.

Ed   Is your fancy man here, as well?

Christopher *gets a set of bongo drums out of one of the boxes. He begins drumming on them. He drums and drums and drums.*

Judy   Christopher.

Christopher.

He's gone. You don't need to panic.

Christopher   Where's he gone to?

Judy   He's gone to stay with Rhodri for a while.

Christopher   Is he going to be arrested? And go to prison?

Judy   What for?

Christopher   For killing Wellington.

Judy   I don't think so. I think he'll only get arrested if Mrs Shears presses charges.

Christopher   What's that?

Judy   It's when you tell the police to arrest somebody for little crimes. They only arrest people for little crimes if you ask them.

Christopher   Is killing Wellington a little crime?

Judy   Yes love it is.

In the next few weeks we're going to try and get a place of our own to live in.

Christopher   Can I do my Maths A-Level?

Judy   You're not listening to me are you, Christopher?

Christopher   I am listening to you.

Judy   I told you. I rang your headmistress. I told her you were in London. I told her you'd do it next year.

Christopher   But I'm here now so I can take it.

Judy   I'm sorry, Christopher. I didn't know we'd be coming back. This isn't going to solve anything.

Mrs Shears   You've got a bloody nerve.

Christopher   Where are we going?

Mrs Shears   Swanning round here as though nothing ever happened.

Judy   Ignore her, Christopher.

Mrs Shears   So has he finally dumped you too?

Christopher   Where are we going?

Mrs Shears   You had it coming. Don't try and pretend that you didn't. Because you bloody did.

Christopher   Where are we going?

Judy   We're going to the school.

Christopher *stops drumming*.

Siobhan   So you're Christopher's mother.

Judy   That's right. And you're . . .

Siobhan   I'm Siobhan. It's nice to meet you.

Judy   Yeah. Yes. Yes. It's nice to meet you too.

Siobhan   Hello Christopher.

Christopher   Hello.

Siobhan   Are you OK?

Christopher   I'm tired.

Judy   He's a bit upset.

Siobhan   Because of the A-Level, you said.

Judy   He won't eat. He won't sleep.

Siobhan   Yeah.

I spoke to Mrs Gascoyne after you called.

Judy   Right.

Siobhan   She still actually has your A-Level papers in the three sealed envelopes in her desk.

Mrs Gascoyne   I still actually have the A-Level papers in my desk.

Christopher   Does that mean I can still do my A-Level?

Siobhan   I think so. We're going to ring the Reverend Peters to make sure he can still come in this afternoon. And Mrs Gascoyne is going to make a call to the examination board to say that you're going to take the exam after all. And hopefully they'll say that that's OK. But we can't know for sure. I thought I should tell you now. So you could think about it.

Christopher   So I could think about what?

Siobhan   Is this what you want to do, Christopher? If you say you don't want to do it no one is going to be angry with you. And it won't be wrong or illegal or stupid. It will just be what you want and that will be fine.

Christopher   I want to do it.

Siobhan   OK.

How tired are you?

Christopher   Very.

Siobhan   How's your brain when you think about maths?

Christopher   I don't think it really works very well.

Siobhan   What's the logarithmic formula for the approximate number of prime numbers not greater than x?

Christopher   I can't think.

Reverend Peters *enters. He picks up one envelope. He opens it. He looks at it. He carefully places it face down on* **Christopher**'s *table.*

He goes to sit opposite him. He takes out a stopwatch.

Reverend Peters   So young man, are we ready to roll?

Christopher *turns over the exam paper.*

He stares at it.

He can't understand any questions. He panics. His breathing becomes erratic. To calm himself he counts the cubes of cardinal numbers.

Christopher   1, 8, 27, 64, 125, 216, 343, 512, 729, 1000, 1331.

Reverend Peters   Are you all right, Christopher?

Christopher   I can't read the question.

Reverend Peters   What do you mean?

Christopher   I can't read the question.

Reverend Peters   Can you see the question?

Christopher   I can see the questions but I can't read the questions because when I look at the words they all seem confused and the wrong way round and mixed up to me.

Reverend Peters   Right.

Christopher   What does this question say?

Reverend Peters   Christopher, I'm afraid I can't help you like that. I'm not allowed to.

Christopher *groans.*

Siobhan   Christopher. Stop groaning. Get your breath. Count the cubes of the cardinal numbers again.

Christopher   1, 8, 27, 64, 125, 216, 343, 512, 729, 1000, 1331.

Siobhan   Now. Have another go.

He looks at the questions again.

Christopher   Show that a triangle with sides that can be written in the form $n^2 + 1$, $n^2 - 1$ and $2n$ (where n is greater than 1) is right-angled.

Siobhan   You don't have to tell us.

Christopher   What?

Siobhan   You don't have to tell us how you solved it.

Christopher   But it's my favourite question.

Siobhan   Yes but it's not very interesting.

Christopher   I think it is.

Siobhan   Christopher, people won't want to hear about the answer to a maths question in a play.

Look, why don't you tell it after the curtain call?

When you've finished you can do a bow and then people who want to can go home and if anybody wants find out how you solved the maths question then they can stay and you can tell them at the end.

OK?

Christopher   OK.

He picks up his pencil.

He starts answering.

Reverend Peters   *Muchas Grazias, mio compadre.* Make sure your name's on the front of the paper. Pop it in here. Don't panic. I'll have a quick word with the big man for you. And let's see what happens, shall we?

Ed *enters.*

Judy *is behind him.*

Ed   Don't scream.

OK, Christopher. I'm not going to hurt you.

Ed *crouches down by* **Christopher**.

I wanted to ask you how the exam went.

Judy   Tell him, Christopher.

Please, Christopher.

Christopher   I don't know if I got all the questions right because I was really tired and I hadn't eaten any food so I couldn't think properly.

Ed *nods. There is some time.*

Ed   Thank you.

Christopher   What for?

Ed   Just . . . thank you. I'm very proud of you, Christopher. Very proud. I'm sure you did really well.

Judy *gives* **Christopher** *the puzzle that she sent him.*

Christopher *successfully solves the puzzle, separating the two parts.*

Siobhan   How's your flat?

Christopher   It's not really a flat. It's a room. It's small. The corridor's painted brown. Other people use the toilet. Mother has to clean the toilet before I can use it. Sometimes there are other people in there so I do wet myself. The corridor smells like gravy and bleach. The room smells like socks and pine air freshener. I don't like waiting for my A-Level result.

If I was living at your house I would have room to put all my things and I wouldn't have to share the toilet with strangers.

Can I come and live in your house so that I'll have room to put all my things and I won't have to share the toilet with strangers?

Siobhan   No, Christopher. You can't.

Christopher   Why can't I? Is it because I'm too noisy and sometimes I'm 'difficult to control'.

Siobhan   No. It's because I'm not your mother, Christopher.

Christopher   No.

Siobhan   That's very important, Christopher. Do you understand that?

Christopher   I don't know.

Mother doesn't get back from work till 5.30. So I have to go to Father's house between 3.49 and 5.30 because I'm not allowed to be on my own. Mother said I didn't have a choice. I pushed the bed up against the door in case Father tries to

come in. Sometimes he tries to talk to me through the door.
I don't answer him. Sometimes he sits outside the door
quietly for a long time.

Ed *enters. He's holding a kitchen timer.*

Ed   Christopher, can I have a talk with you?

Christopher *turns away from* **Siobhan**.

Christopher   No. No. No. No. No. No, you can't. No.

Judy   It's OK. I'll be here.

Christopher   I don't want to talk to Father.

Ed   I'll do you a deal. Five minutes, OK? That's all. Then
you can go.

Ed *sets the timer for five minutes. It starts ticking.*

Christopher, look . . . Things can't go on like this. I don't
know about you, but this . . . this just hurts too much. You
being in the house but refusing to talk to me. You have to
learn to trust me . . . And I don't care how long it takes . . . if
it's a minute one day and two minutes the next and three
minutes the next and it takes years I don't care. Because this
is important. This is more important than anything else.
Let's call it . . . let's call it a project. A project we have to do
together. You have to spend more time with me. And I . . . I
have to show you that you can trust me. And it will be
difficult at first because . . . because it's a difficult project.
But it will get better, I promise. You don't have to say
anything, not right now. You have to think about it. And . . .
I've got you a present. To show you that I really mean what I
say. And to say sorry. And because . . . well you'll see what I
mean.

Ed *leaves.*

*He comes back with a big cardboard box. It is importantly cardboard
and different to the other boxes. There's a blanket in it. He puts his*

hands in the box. He takes out a little sandy-coloured Golden Retriever.

He's two months old.

The dog sits on **Christopher***'s lap.*

Judy   You won't be able to take him away with you, I'm afraid. The bedsit's too small. But your father's going to look after him here. And you can come and take him out for walks whenever you want.

Christopher   Does he have a name?

Ed   No. You can decide what to call him.

Christopher   Sandy. He's called Sandy.

The alarm goes off.

They look at each other.

Judy   We need to go now.

Ed   Yes.

Judy   We'll come back tomorrow and you can see him then.

Siobhan   Christopher.

Christopher   Yes.

Siobhan   Here.

Christopher   What's this?

Siobhan   It's your result, Christopher.

Christopher   Right.

Siobhan   You need to open it and read it.

Christopher   Right.

He does.

Siobhan   Well? What does it say?

Christopher   I got an A.

Siobhan   Oh. Oh. That's just. That's terrific, Christopher.

Christopher   Yes.

Siobhan   Aren't you happy?

Christopher   Yes. It's the best result.

Siobhan   I know it is. How's your dog?

Christopher   He's very well. I stayed last week at Father's because Mother got flu and he slept on my bed so he can bark in case anybody comes into my room at night.

Siobhan   Right. How are you getting on with your father, Christopher?

Christopher   He planted a vegetable patch in his garden. I helped him and Sandy watched. We planted carrots and peas and spinach and I'm going to pick them when they're ready. He bought me a book, which is called *Further Maths for A-Level*. He told Mrs Gascoyne that I'm going to take Further Maths next year. She said OK.

Mrs Gascoyne   OK.

Siobhan   I heard that.

Christopher   I'm going to pass it and get an A grade. And then in two years I'll take A-Level Physics and get an A grade. And then I'm going to go to university in another town. It doesn't have to be in London because I don't like London and there are universities in lots of places and not all of them are in big cities. I can live in a flat with a garden and a proper toilet. I can take Sandy and my books and my computer. Then I will get a First-Class Honours degree. Then I will be a scientist. I can do these things.

Siobhan   I hope so.

Christopher   I can because I went to London on my own.

She looks at him.

I solved the mystery of Who Killed Wellington.

She looks at him.

I found my mother. I was brave.

Siobhan   You were.

Christopher   And I wrote a book.

Siobhan   I know. I read it. We turned it into a play.

Christopher   Yes. Does that mean I can do anything, do you think?

Does that mean I can do anything, Siobhan?

Does that mean I can do anything?

The two look at each other for a while.

Lights black.

After the curtain call **Christopher** *returns to the stage. He gets the attention of anybody still in the audience.*

Postscript

Christopher   Thank you very much for clapping and thank you very much for staying behind to listen to how I answered the question on my Maths A-level. Siobhan said it wouldn't be very interesting but I said it was.

She didn't tell me what I should use, so I decided to use everything in the theatre including VL000 arc lights, which are moving lights, a smoke machine, light-emitting diodes, UBL control speakers, an overhead projector and a woman called a deputy stage manager who will operate these.

The lights referred to should be the actual lights used in the production and these references should change accordingly.

I had ninety minutes to answer ten questions – but I spent thirty minutes doing groaning which meant I only had six minutes to answer this question.

A timer may be projected, displaying 6.00.00.

And this is what I wrote.

Christopher *starts the timer. A right-angled triangle, made using lasers, might float above* **Christopher** *and slowly lower around him. If this is not possible the triangle could be made by projection or by the company.*

'Prove the following:

'A triangle with sides that can be written in the form $n^2 + 1$, $n^2 - 1$ and $2n$ (where n is bigger than 1) is right-angled.'

If the triangle is right-angled, one of its angles will be 90 degrees and will therefore follow Pythagoras's theorem.

According to Pythagoras:
(*Company sing/rap/* **Christopher** *with delay.*)
If the sum of the squares of the two shorter sides
Equals the square of the hypotenuse
Then the triangle is
Then the triangle is
Then the triangle is
Right-angled.

Pythagoras said that $a^2 + b^2 = c^2$.

To put it simply, if you draw squares outside the three sides of a right-angled triangle, then add up the area of the two smaller squares, this will be equal to the area of the larger square. This is only true if the triangle is a right-angled triangle.

A projected diagram may show this at this point.

The A-level question is an algebraic formula for making right-angled triangles. Algebra is like a computer programme that works for whatever numbers you put into it.

I have to show that a triangle with sides whose lengths are $n^2 + 1$, $n^2 - 1$ and $2n$ (where n is bigger than 1) is right-angled.

To find the area of the squares you have to multiply one of the sides by itself. I must show that the area of the squares on the two shorter sides adds up to the square on the long side.

This means doing some algebra.

A formula representing the necessary mathematical equation may appear at this point.

Let me show you.

He refers to the demonstrated triangle.

> To find the area of $2n$, we simply multiply $2n$
> by $2n$. This equals $4n^2$.

He refers to the triangle again.

*As he solves the problem so any demonstration of triangle or
equation might change to follow the solution.*

> To find the area of $n^2 - 1$, we must multiply
> $n^2 - 1$ by $n^2 - 1$.
>
> I will draw lines on the equation to show
> what is multiplied.
>
> (Stupid people at my school get very
> confused at this point. Although I am not
> allowed to call them stupid even though that
> is what they are.)
>
> That gives me n to the power of four $- 2n^2 +$
> 1.
>
> Now I must add these together:
>
> n to the power of $4 + 4n^2 - 2n^2 + 1 = n$ to the
> power of $4 + 2n^2 + 1$.
>
> If the triangle is right-angled, this answer
> should be equal to the area of the larger
> square. Let's check:
>
> $n^2 + 1 \times n^2 + 1 = n$ to power of $4 + 2n^2 + 1$.
>
> So the areas of the two small squares add
> up to the area of the large square. So all my
> squares fit together to satisfy Pythagoras's
> theorem. So the triangle is right-angled.
>
> Now let's check this proof with some
> examples:
>
> If $n = 2$, the triangle has lengths 3, 4 and 5,
> and $3^2 + 4^2$ is $9 + 16$ which is 25 which is 5^2.

If $n = 3$, the sides of the triangle are 8, 6 and 10, and $8^2 + 6^2$ is $64 + 36$ which is 100 which is 10^2.

$n = 4$: the sides of the triangle are 15, 8 and 17, and $15^2 + 8^2$ is $225 + 64$ which is 289 which is 17^2.

$n = 5$: the sides of the triangle are 24, 10 and 26, and $24^2 + 10^2$ is $576 + 100$ which is 676 which is 26^2.

$n = 6$: the sides of the triangle are 35, 12 and 37, and $35^2 + 12^2$ is $1225 + 144$ which is 1369 which is 37^2.

My proof shows why this works for every n.

Quod erat demonstrandum.

And that is how I got an A grade!!!

The Curious Incident of the Dog in the Night-Time: Teaching and learning activities

Developing literary analysis

The structured active learning approaches outlined in the scheme of work enable pupils to build their learning and construct their understanding. Pupils are required to use drama activities to:

♦ Analyse writers' complex techniques and skills

♦ Understand texts in a cultural and historical context

♦ Understand writers' intentions and choices of language, structures and ideas

♦ Analyse the different contributions made by novelists, playwrights, directors, narrators

♦ Analyse images, drama and literary techniques

Analytical writing

Such work has a direct effect on pupils' ability to write about literary and dramatic techniques and use evidence from the text to back up their ideas. Integrated within the work are, therefore, suggestions for further analytical work. It is important that the drama activities are not seen as separate from these – they should complement each other. Discussions and written work should be directly informed by drama work, resulting in a more detailed analysis and understanding of the text and of the dramatic/ literary process.

Structuring the activities

The use of drama conventions in isolation will not produce deep learning opportunities. The 'learning' section of the scheme of work is devised in such a way that pupils build their learning and are provided with the appropriate contexts and techniques to produce high-level responses and skills. Sharing such an approach with the pupils allows them to have an understanding of 'the bigger picture', vital if they are to become independent, active learners. The scheme of work is addressed directly to the pupils so that they can understand and analyse the learning process and consider the progress they are making in each of the skills identified. While individual activities are identified within the scheme, they are often interlinked and interdependent and are best approached within the complete scheme of work. Similarly, lesson breaks are not identified, as these will be dependent on the length of lessons and nature of the learning groups involved.

Resources

All the resources required are identified in the scheme of work. Some preparation time is required to ensure that these are available when required. For example the items required for activities (string, hoops, bongo drums, etc.) can, when not readily available, be purchased cheaply or substituted. For ease of use, a laptop and multi-media projector will enable extracts of the text and maps to be projected on to a screen for pupils to see. If a multi-media projector is not available, then the use of an overhead projector is also effective for presenting images and text. Film soundtracks provide effective music to be used during the activities but other appropriate music, without lyrics, can be used in the places identified, as can the bongo drums referenced in the script. Copies of the quotations and the extract from the novel are available on the Methuen Drama website:

www.bloomsbury.com/criticalscripts

Use of space

While some of the activities benefit from a more open environment that allows for a flexible use of floor space, tables and chairs, a drama studio or large space is not required. If space is limited, a classroom can easily be adjusted to enable all the activities to take place.

1. Introducing and exploring ideas

To analyse text and introduce key ideas within the play.

Learning	Teaching & Resources
✦ The whole class (divided in half) sits in two large circles, surrounding two inner circles of words (written/printed individually on to pieces of card). The words, if rearranged, make two quotations from the script.	▪ The word-cards need to be prepared before the lesson and set out (in a random order) within two separate circles.
✦ Around the room will be quotations from the play ('I promise', 'Do you know that it is wrong to lie', If you don't tell the truth now, then later on it hurts even more') and mathematical equations, questions and prime numbers ('864×251', '157, 163, 167, 173, 17', 'Show that a triangle with sides that can be written in the form $n^2 + 1$, $n^2 - 1$ and $2n$ (where n is greater than 1) is right-angled'.)	The quotations need to be prepared before the lesson (see website).

- Read out all the words around the circle, thinking carefully about the order the words might go in, so that they make sense as one quotation. Through discussion and negotiation, reposition the words around the circle so that they can be read out in the 'correct' order. Everyone listens to both quotations being read.

- As a class, sit in a large semi-circle facing the projected quotations and discuss what they mean and why they might be important to the text.

- Look at the projected image of a Venn diagram with the quotations printed within each circle. Discuss which words or ideas suggested by either quotation could be placed in the central overlap? Why?

'The word metaphor means carrying something from one place to another and it is when you describe something by using a word for something that it isn't.'

'I don't like acting because it is pretending that something is real when it is not really real at all so it is like a kind of lie.

- ▣ Project the quotations

- ▣ Project a Venn Diagram

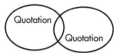

✦ Discuss what the quotations and numbers around the room suggest about the play you are about to explore.

✦ Speaking and Listening – Discuss the strategies used to negotiate the 'correct' order and the clues you used to formulate a response.

✦ How might a Venn diagram be used to explore characters, themes or ideas in the play?

✦ How and why might the playwright focus on the use of metaphors, pretence and lies to convey ideas to the audience?

2. Introducing a context and a character

To develop a context and reflect on the techniques used to introduce the characters and key ideas.

Learning	Teaching & Resources
✦ Sit in a large semi-circle facing the projected image. Watch the short film clip. What have you noticed about the shots in this clip? What sort of landscape is it?	◾ YouTube clip http://www.youtube.com /watch?v=C9GzipgQCJA
✦ In groups of four, you are going to develop a Commentary to accompany these shots, describing what can be seen out of the train window. Try to include	The texts (taken from pages 57–58 of the script) need to be prepared before the lesson, as do stills from the film clip.

metaphors in your Commentary. Each group will be allocated a slightly different section and be given a still from the film as a guide. You will also be given some pieces of 'text' that would be found inside the train, that you are going to introduce in to your Commentary.

✦ Using your still as a stimulus, develop a Commentary (spoken in first person in the present tense) that describes what you can see. At different stages in your Commentary, other members of the group will interrupt by reading out loud one of the texts found within the carriage.

✦ Move in to a space with your group next to a picture. You will be given some time to rehearse your Commentary in your groups before the process begins.

✦ Stand with your group in a large circle. When the music fades, the first group will step forward as the teacher freezes the film, and provide the Commentary until the music begins again. The next group will then move forward. This

Model how this could be done by commentating on a short piece of the film clip and reading out a poster that could be displayed in the carriage.

Copies of the stills from the film clip should be placed round the room.

Use the 'frame forward' command at this stage to control the shots displayed.

♫ Music.

▣ Extract from the film clip.

will continue until all groups have provided Commentaries of the scene from the train and verbalised the texts found within the train carriage.

✦ When all the groups have provided Commentaries, the teacher will read the following extract,

Extract 1 (page 65)

From **Christopher:** 1. There are nineteen cows in the field.

to 7. The cows are mostly facing uphill.

Further activities, reflection, analysis or discussion

✦ Discuss how the use of commentary or verbalising texts might be used within the play. Why?

✦ Discuss what Christopher's description tells us about him? What are the playwright's aims here?

✦ What differences are created by the description that includes metaphors and the description that Christopher uses? How might the playwright develop this in the play?

✦ Discuss the front cover of the play and what it suggests about the content and themes of the play.

3. Investigating the opening scenes and structure

To investigate and analyse the text and reflect on the techniques used to introduce the characters and key ideas.

Learning	Teaching & Resources
✦ You will be working in a small group of between 2 and 5 students. Each group is given an extract from pages 3–16 of the play. (See extracts below.)	By exploring these extracts, the pupils begin to select and analyse the relevant information. They also begin to take a real interest in the material and want to know more. By Action Reading the extracts, they have to consider some of the initial issues that directors and actors need to address.

Extract 1 (Pages 3–4)

From The start of the play

to *Christopher looks at the Policeman.*

Extract 2 (Pages 4–6)

From I do not tell lies.

to And it can also mean 'I think what you just said was very stupid'.

Extract 3 (Pages 6–8)

From Could you take your laces out of your shoes please, Christopher?

to Right. Lovely. Do you know your father's phone number, Christopher?

By working on the different extracts in this way, and sharing them with the class through Rolling Theatre, they are essentially teaching each other different aspects of

Extract 4 (Pages 8–10)

From Christopher turns to Ed. Ed looks at him.

to Do you understand what I'm saying? Yes.

Extract 5 (Pages 10–12)

From The second main reason is that people often talk using metaphors.

to Yes, Christopher, you could say that. You could very well say that.

Extract 6 (Pages 12–14)

From Siobhan reads more from the book.

to If I make her a get-well card will you take it in for her tomorrow?

Extract 7 (Pages 14–15)

From How are you today, Christopher?

to I don't know.

Extract 8 (Pages 15–16)

From Christopher, if your father's told you not to do something maybe you shouldn't do it.

to If you don't go now I will call the police again.

the script. It is, therefore, not necessary to read large amounts of the script as a whole class. This more active approach leads to engagement and deeper levels of understanding and analysis.

✦ In your group, produce a short Digital Video Clip of the extract. To do this, you begin with a Still Image, followed by an Action Reading of the script and then freeze at the end in a final Still Image. You need to investigate the script and search for clues about the characters, story and setting in order to produce an accurate Action Reading of the extract.

For each of the Still Images, stop the pupils (by counting them down using the prime numbers from 11, 7, 5, 3 and 2) while they are 'rehearsing' and ask them to show the Still Images. Once they have all frozen, ask them to sharpen the pictures to show the tension.

✦ As a class, you produce your Digital Video Clips as Rolling Theatre. Music is used to guide you. All the groups freeze in their initial Still Image and then the first group unfreezes, adds the action and then freezes again. When they freeze, the next group knows that they can begin. This continues with all the groups producing their Digital Video Clip, until all groups have shown their pieces. When you are not presenting your Digital Video Clip, you can become a Spect-actor. This means that while your body remains frozen in the Still Image, your head can turn to follow the action so that you can see and hear the

Position the groups round the room according to the order of the *extracts*.

♫ Play music at the start, end and in between each extract.

Remind them of the nature of Spect-acting and the importance of freezing in their final Still Images at the end of the Rolling Theatre.

work of the other groups. You should remain in your place, in order for all the groups to freeze in their final Still Image at the end.

✦ Reflecting on the scenes that you have just presented and observed, think about the structure of the play and the devices the playwright has used. How do you ensure smooth transitions between and within the different extracts when the action moves from one scene to another or where Siobhan's reading provides a character's voice? What techniques could you add to ensure the audience understand what is happening. Discuss this within your group and with the groups either side of your extract.

To model this process, you might provide examples of different ways of developing a transition or scene such as: Siobhan having a book that she is reading from, the other groups turning to face the action as it happens; Siobhan being removed from each group and placed in the centre of the circle.

✦ As a class, re-run the Rolling Theatre adding the techniques and/or devices that you have discussed.

♫ Play music at the start, end and in between each extract.

Further activities, reflection, analysis or discussion

✦ How did the Rolling Theatre activity help you to analyse and understand the significance of the scenes and explore the methods used to introduce the audience to the different characters and issues?

✦ How did the changes made to the Rolling Theatre help your understanding of the scenes? What techniques do you think the playwright, director and actors would have used?

✦ What role does Siobhan have throughout these scenes and how do you think this relates to the decisions the playwright made when adapting the novel in to a play?

✦ Discuss what is understood by 'Truth' and how this is explored in the opening scenes. What attitude does the audience have towards the characters at this stage of the play and what ideas do they expect to be explored throughout the play? Why?

✦ Preparing for written analytical responses. Analyse how the language devices and techniques are used to explore:

    ✦ Characters
    ✦ Relationships
    ✦ Tension
    ✦ A sense of voice

4. Placing the playwright and writer

To analyse the significance of characters' conscience and sense of responsibility in the play and the different techniques used by the writer to explore the characters' reactions and thoughts.

Learning	Teaching & Resources
✦ Stand in a large circle or semi-circle with sight of the text (projected or as individual copies). As a class, read the extract from the play, pages 30–32 (and all the stage instructions).	▣ It is helpful to project the text and have individual copies of the extract for the students.
from Why did you say 'I think you know why your father doesn't like Mr Shears very much'?	
to Ed goes to Siobhan. He looks at her holding the book. He reaches his hand out for it. After a short time she passes it to him.	
✦ Members of the class are given the roles of Christopher, Siobhan and Ed. Using the space in the centre of the circle, Sculpt them into the scene at this point. You will need to consider their frozen positions, facial expressions and gestures. Other members of the class might adjust the positions until a final sculpture is agreed. The characters freeze.	Ensure that the sculpted positions are supported with evidence from the text. Give value to the different positions offered by explaining that the director at different points in the scene could have used these positions.

- The teacher will stand between two of the characters and indicate the space between them. Describe the space between the characters. You might suggest various alternatives – 'The space of concern, fear, etc.'

When asking about the 'space', actually stand in that space so the students can visualise it.

- The teacher will choose a student to take the role of the 'playwright' (Simon Stephens) and ask them to hold the 'Playwright' card. Place the Playwright in the Sculpted Image where you think he should be. You might use various criteria for this, including the playwright's distance from certain characters, the empathy created, the events, the writer's intention and what role Siobhan has. Justify your choices, using evidence from the text to support your ideas. Discuss the positioning as a class. Throughout this discussion, other students should demonstrate the position they feel is most appropriate by moving and Placing the Playwright and justifying their choice.

🖆 Props (to be used throughout the unit of work). Four large pieces of card with 'Audience', 'Playwright', 'Writer' and 'Reader' printed on them.

Ask specific questions such as 'Which character is the writer closest to in terms of empathy or the sympathy created?' 'What/who is the playwright trying to control most in this scene?'

It is important that the students physically move the playwright, before justifying why.

◆ As a class, read the extract from the novel, which covers the same scene. Page 94 to page 95 and page 100 to page 101.

▣ Project the text.

from That night I wrote some more of my book and the next morning I took it into school.

to So I would be feeling sad about something that isn't real and doesn't exist. And that would be stupid.

And

Stop at appropriate places throughout the reading to discuss any differences between the novel and play and the techniques used by the playwright and novelist.

from When I got home from school Father was still out at work . . .

to I had forgotten that I had left my book lying on the kitchen table because I was too interested in the *Blue Planet* video. This is what is called Relaxing your Guard and it is what you must never do if you are a detective.

♫ Play music in between the lines to structure the work and help develop the sense of tension.

◆ Using the space in the centre of the circle, Sculpt the characters of Ed and Christopher into the scene at this point in the novel.

It is important that you select different students to those Sculpted before.

- Another student is chosen to be the 'writer' of the novel (Mark Haddon). Position or Place the Writer in the frozen scene where you think he should be. Discuss the positioning as a class. Throughout the discussion, other students should demonstrate the position they feel is most appropriate by moving and Placing the Writer and justifying their choice.

Discuss any differences in the position of the writer of the novel compared with that of the playwright. What reasons are there for this?

- Return to the Sculpted scene from the play and position it in the circle alongside the Sculpted scene from the novel. Discuss how the positions of the Playwright and Writer differ/are similar? Why?

Encourage the students to refer to specific details and techniques in both the novel and the play to support their arguments.

- The characters and writers freeze, while the teacher stands behind the novelist, looks at the Playwright and introduces a provocative phrase such as, 'You should have just let Ed discover the book. This scene's not right.'

- You will be asked what you think the playwright would say, how Mark Haddon the novelist might respond and what other comments the

It should be clear that there is no 'right' answer. Students are developing their understanding of the writers' techniques and how key ideas are explored throughout

writer or playwright might make about this scene. Discuss this with the person standing next to you and as a whole class.

✦ The teacher will explain that the sculpted scenes (see diagram) will freeze and the 'writer' and 'playwright' will leave the scenes and begin a journey in different directions around the circle. As the 'writer' and the 'playwright' take turns, taking one step at a time around the circle, they will hear their responses, comments and explanations about this scene that the playwright and writer themselves might think and say.

✦ The teacher repeats the provocative phrase, 'You should have just let Ed discover the book. This scene's not right.' As the playwright steps in front of a student in the circle, the student will respond to this statement as if they were the playwright. The writer will then take a step around the circle in the opposite direction (see diagram) and the student he is closest to makes a further comment or asks a question.

these scenes in the novel and in the play.

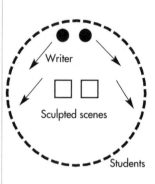

Modelling of this process will need to take place before the activity begins.

This process continues as the 'writer' and 'playwright' make their way round the circle and the students speak the thoughts, comments and questions

✦ When the students in role as the writer and playwright meet at the opposite side of the circle, the teacher will again repeat the opening line and the 'playwright' and 'writer' will themselves continue the conversation, supported by the ideas and comments they have been given as they made their way round the circle.

✦ The teacher will ask the characters to freeze and will read the following extract from the play (pages 34–35).

> **Ed** What is this?
>
> *Christopher looks at Ed.*
>
> **Ed** Jesus, Christopher, how stupid are you? What the hell did I tell you, Christopher? . . .
>
> *Ed grabs Christopher's arm.*
>
> *Christopher screams.*
>
> *Ed shakes Christopher hard with both hands.*

Due to the nature of this activity, it is important that the students who take on the roles of writer and playwright are selected carefully.

Christopher punches Ed repeatedly in the face. He cuts his mouth.

Ed hits the side of Christopher's head.

Christopher falls unconscious for a few seconds.

Ed stands above him. He is still holding the book.

✦ Read the comments by Simon Stephens and Mark Haddon about their roles as writers and their views on this scene. As a class, discuss whether the position of the writers or their responses would now change. Why?

Comments from Mark Haddon

The novel is set inside Christopher's head. We see the world around him but we see it only through his eyes. The irony is that we always understand that world better than he does. We understand all the clues he sees and misreads (in this scene, for example, we know exactly why his father doesn't like Mr Shears very much). He is an unreliable narrator. But he is reliably unreliable. We very quickly learn to decode what he's telling us. We are always one step ahead.

Drama, however, is always in the third person. We never truly get inside a character's head. We hear their words and look at their body and have to work out what they are thinking and feeling. And this problem was always going to be a difficult one for anyone adapting the play for the stage – how to turn a first-person narrative into a third-person script, how to tell the story from outside Christopher's head without losing something really important about his peculiar view of the world from inside it.

In the play we don't get to play the game of putting together a picture of Christopher's world using only the clues he gives us. On the other hand the characters we see in the novel only through Christopher's eyes are suddenly right there in front of us, as real as Christopher himself. Their words, their actions, their feelings now have equal weight. They affect us directly.

The big emotional turning point in the centre of the novel is when Christopher discovers his mother's letters. This is when his view of the world is shattered. The book that he is writing matters less. It is mostly a way for us to eavesdrop on his thoughts, for Siobhan to eavesdrop on his thoughts and, ultimately, for his father to eavesdrop on his thoughts.

On stage this is reversed and the book becomes a very dangerous object. When Christopher discovers the letters we have to imagine his pain, but when Ed reads the book we know that something awful is going to happen and that we are about to watch two people badly hurting one another.

Should Ed take the book from Siobhan's hands as in Simon's script? It's a moment which dramatises an idea. It's metaphorical. Christopher would never put something like that in a play. After all, it didn't happen! But whose play are we watching? Is it Christopher's or Simon's?

Come to think of it, whose novel were we reading, Christopher's or mine?

Comments from Simon Stephens

Mark's book is a book about writing a book. When it came to dramatising it I realised that there was something potentially very dramatic about the actual book that Christopher, the imaginary character Mark created, was writing. His book works a bit like a diary. People who keep diaries often keep them secret. They are hot property. To have them discovered can be embarrassing or exposing or hurtful. But certainly it can be dramatic. I wanted to create that drama around the book.

It struck me that two other people apart from Christopher read his book. These are Siobhan and Ed. And their reading of the book is more dramatic than Christopher's because they understand things he doesn't. Siobhan understands the nature of betrayal and affairs in marriages. Ed understands that Christopher is starting to discover things not just about the murder of Wellington but about the secrets he's kept from his son.

I realised that Siobhan would want to protect Christopher from the consequences of Ed finding the book. At that moment she would understand what Christopher couldn't but the audience does. There is a dramatic irony to any moment in a play where audiences understand more than characters do, that is very satisfying. She would want to protect him. But also she would have to defer to Ed. She is, importantly, *not* Christopher's parent. Teachers can't replace parents. *No* matter how much she wants to protect Christopher she can't overrule Ed.

I wanted to physicalise this moment.

The moment that Ed discovers the book is one of my favourite moments in the play. It raises the question 'Where are we?' And 'When are we?' Are we in Christopher's classroom? Are we on the beach at Polperro? Are we at home with Ed discovering the book? This multiplicity of perspective is very typical of Mark's writing and very typical of the way Christopher thinks. I wanted to find a stage language that dramatised that.

As it happens in the original production at the National the director Marianne Elliot chose not to have Ed take the book from Siobhan but rather just to find it.

Clearly she agreed with the teacher!

Further activities, reflection, analysis or discussion

✦ How does the playwright explore the tension in this scene, through specific linguistic and dramatic devices?

✦ Detailed analysis of these extracts from the novel and play, together with the writers' comments, enables an exploration of the different roles the writers, director and actors play in interpreting the script and presenting ideas, tensions and relationships.

✦ Compare the different arguments presented to explore writers' ideas and perspectives. Explain and evaluate how the writer and playwright use linguistic, grammatical, structural and presentational features to achieve effects and engage and influence the reader/audience.

✦ Analyse what dramatic and literary techniques are used to present perspective, a sense of voice and/or a character's conscience/inner thoughts.

✦ How have the drama activities helped to develop these analytical skills?

5. Revealing and exploring 'truths'

To explore the tension in the play and investigate and analyse the text and question critically the ideas and issues introduced.

Learning

✦ As a class, read the extract from the play when Christopher is searching for his book (pages 37 and 38).

✦ Sculpt the scene in Ed's bedroom at the point when Christopher says:

It was an envelope addressed to me and it was lying under my book in the shirt box with some other envelopes. I picked it up.

✦ Sculpt Christopher into the scene at this point. Read on:

from Christopher finds the envelope

to I only know three people who do little circles instead of dots over the letter i. And one of them is Siobhan. And one of them was Mr Loxley who used to teach at the school. And one of them was Mother.

✦ The teacher will hold up the envelope and ask what you think would be inside. Suggest what written text you think would be inside and, as

Teaching & Resources

◼ Project the text.

✎ Props – shirt box, letters, other items from the room.

◼ Project the text.

Ask the students to place the props first to establish a setting before sculpting the character in to the scene.

◼ It is helpful to project the text.

✎ Prop – envelope with the address written as described.

a whole class, discuss other possibilities.

✦ In groups of four, create the text that could appear in the envelope. It is important that you create two identical versions of this piece of text. You will need to think about what you know about the play so far and the characters that are involved.

✦ When you have completed the piece of text, place it in an envelope. Set up the Sculpted Scene again and, one at a time, place the envelopes into the shirt box. Keep the other copy of the text, as you will be reading it out later when the scene is 'brought to life'. You will need to think about how it might be read. What tone should be used? Should there be pauses?

✦ You continue to work in the same group. Each group is given an extract from one of the letters in the play:

Extract 1 (Pages 43–44)

From 451c Chapter Road, London

to I liked remembering that a lot.

✎ Prop – blank pieces of paper and pens.

At this stage it is useful to discuss as a whole class what is known about Christopher's mother and the events that might have taken place.

✎ Prop – envelopes. These could be colour-coded or numbered to identify which group they belong to.

♬ Play music as the envelopes are being placed.

Colour-coding and numbering the extracts ensures that you can maintain the chronological order throughout the activity.

Extract 2 (Pages 44–45)

From Dear Christopher. I said I
        wanted to explain to you

to   and I tried to pick you up and
        move you.

Extract 3 (Page 45)

From And everyone turned round
        to see what was going on

to   I knew you wouldn't go on
        the bus again.

Extract 4 (Page 45)

From And I remember that night I
        just cried

to   And that was when I started
        spending lots of time with
        Roger.

Extract 5 (Page 46)

From And that was when I started
        spending lots of time with
        Roger.

to   and you threw it and it hit
        my foot and broke my toes.

Extract 6 (Pages 46–47)

From And afterwards at home your
        father and I had a huge
        argument.

to   And so I said yes.

Extract 7 (Page 47)

From And I meant to say goodbye.

to   I thought I was doing the best for all of us.

Extract 8 (Page 47)

From I used to have dreams that everything would get better.

to   He said that if you managed it you were a genius.

♦ In your group, produce a short Digital Video Clip that brings the scene(s) described in the letter to life. To do this, you begin with a Still Image, followed by a short acted scene of the events/memories described in the letter, with speech and movement, and then freeze at the end in a final Still Image.

Now that they are familiar with this technique, encourage them to develop the roles and the use of tension in the Still Images and acted scenes.

♦ As a class, you will now produce the readings of the letters and the Digital Video Clips of the letters from the script as Rolling Theatre.

You will need to provide enough time for the groups to rehearse their reading of their own crafted text and the Digital Video Clips of extracts from the scripted letters.

♦ Set up the sculpted character of Christopher with the shirt box in the centre of the circle. All the groups freeze in their initial Still Image. The student in role as

This needs to be modelled before the process begins.

Christopher will 'come to life', pick up the first letter and then freeze. One member of the first group, that placed this particular piece of text, will step out of the Still Image and read it out, using the retained copy. S/he will then step back in to the Still Image and the group 'come to life', adding the action that depicts the scene from their particular letter in the playscript and then freeze again. When they freeze, the student in role as Christopher will pick up the next letter from the box and the next group knows that they can begin. This continues with all the groups producing their readings of their own text and the Digital Video Clips of the letters in the playscript, until all groups have shown their pieces. When you are not presenting your Digital Video Clip, you can become a Spect-actor. You should remain in your place, in order for all the groups to freeze in their final Still Image at the end.

♪ Play music at the start, end and in between each extract.

It is important that you select the right student to maintain the role of Christopher. A Teaching Assistant or the teacher can also take on this role.

✦ The teacher will pick up all the letters in the shirt box, tie them into a bundle with a piece of string and return them to the box. S/he will then read the following extract from the play:

Christopher's thrashing has exhausted him. He has been sick. He lies still for a while, wrapped in a ball. The box of his mother's letters is next to him.

Ed Christopher? Christopher?

Christopher doesn't respond.

Ed Christopher, what the hell are you doing?

☞ Prop – string.

Further activities, reflection, analysis or discussion

✦ Analyse the use of dramatic devices to build tension and develop the audience's understanding of the characters' motivations.

✦ Discuss and model how the skills demonstrated both in and out of role could be transferred to analytical responses about the writer's techniques and the effect of the text on the reader.

✦ If the playwright and audience were positioned in this scene at moments of tension or revelation, where would they be?

6. Exploring and analysing text and truths

To analyse how promises, lies, truths and facts become key features of the text and how the playwright encourages the audience to explore these.

Learning	Teaching & Resources

Learning

✦ Working in a small group of between 2 and 5 students you will be given an extract from the play that explores lies, promises and truth.

Extract 1 (Pages 9–10)

From Did you mean to hit the policeman?

to Do you understand what I'm saying?

Extract 2 (Pages 23–24)

From I have just had a phone call from Mrs Shears.

to And you know what it means when I make you promise.

Extract 3 (Pages 49–50)

From How are you feeling? Can I get you anything?

to It's going to be all right. Honestly. Trust me.

Extract 4 (Pages 54–55)

From Christopher, what on earth has happened to you?

Teaching & Resources

By working on the different extracts in this way, and sharing them with the class through Rolling Theatre, they are essentially teaching each other different aspects of the script. It is, therefore, not necessary to read large amounts of the script as a whole class. This more active approach leads to engagement and deeper levels of understanding and analysis.

These extracts should enable students to apply their knowledge of the

to And I'm sure that there's been a dreadful misunderstanding.

Extract 5 (Page 63)

From Christopher. Caught you. Just in time.

to I think you've done enough adventuring for one day.

Extract 6 (Pages 79–80)

From You're very brave.

to It's not your fault.

Extract 7 (Pages 80–81)

From Will you let him take me away?

to He told Christopher I was dead.

Extract 8 (Page 83)

From It's OK, Christopher, I won't let him do anything. You're all right.

to You go back to sleep now. Everything is going to be all right. I promise.

Extract 9 (Page 90–91)

From You think you're so bloody clever, don't you?

to We're going home.

playwright's techniques and explore how tension and dramatic impact can be developed.

✦ In your group, produce a Digital Video Clip of the extract. (See Activity 3.)

✦ As a class, you produce your Digital Video Clips as Rolling Theatre. Music is used to guide you. All the groups freeze in their initial Still Image. One member of the first group will collect from the centre of the circle the bundle of letters used in the previous exercise and place the bundle where they feel it is most appropriate in their Still Image. Then the first group 'comes to life', adds the action and then freezes again. When they freeze, the next group knows that they can begin by collecting the bundle of letters, placing it in their Still Image and 'coming to life'. This continues with all the groups collecting and placing the bundle of letters and producing their Digital Video Clips, until all groups have shown their pieces. When you are not presenting your Digital Video Clip, you can become a Spect-actor.

For each of the Still Images, stop the pupils (by counting them down in prime numbers from 11, 7, 5, 3 to 2) while they are 'rehearsing' and ask them to show the Still Images. Once they have all frozen, ask them to sharpen the pictures to show the tension.

Remind them of the nature of Spect-acting and the importance of freezing in their final Still Images at the end of the Rolling Theatre.

Each group will need to decide who will collect the bundle of letters and where they are to place it in the first Still Image.

♪ Use bongo drums, as referenced in the text, loudly at the start, end and in between each extract and quietly during the extracts. Try to create the rhythm of a heartbeat and/or train throughout with the drums.

✦ Reflecting on the extract that you have just presented, decide as a group, what is the most significant line in your extract. Select the line and copy it on to a piece of card. Produce two Still Images to accompany two readings of the line. The first Still Image should be a literal interpretation of the line as it appears in the play. The second Still Image should provide a symbolic interpretation or depiction of the subtext of the line. You will need to also consider where the bundle of letters will be placed in each of the Still Images.

To model the process, examples of different lines and their subtext should be discussed and how these could be presented through Still Images.

✦ All the groups will hold their first Still Image. The first group places the letters in their Still Image and then says the line from the extract, thinking carefully how they will do this. Once they have finished, the next group will know they can begin, collecting and placing the letters and saying the line. This process will continue until all the groups have held the Still Images and spoken the lines. All the groups will then merge into

♫ Use bongo drums drums, as described above, throughout the process.

their 'subtext' Still Images and the Rolling Theatre process will be repeated. You will need to consider how the line could be said differently this time to reveal/emphasise more of the subtext?

✦ Once the Rolling Theatre is complete, the teacher will take the letters from the last Still Image, undo the string and scatter the letters in the centre of the circle while saying

> A dead dog lies in the middle of the stage. A large garden fork is sticking out of its side.
>
> Christopher Boone, fifteen years old, stands on one side of it. His forty-two-year-old neighbour Mrs Shears stands on the other.
>
> They stand for a while without saying anything. The rest of the company watch, waiting to see who is going to dare to speak first.

All students need to hold their Still Images at the end. Music can be played to assist with this.

Further activities, reflection, analysis or discussion

+ Discuss how this activity has helped you to analyse the subtexts of the play. What techniques have been used by the playwright to build tension in these scenes and suggest there are hidden truths and thoughts that the audience needs to understand?

+ Analyse the use of dramatic devices to build tension and layers of meaning, which develop the audience's understanding.

+ Discuss the importance of the playwright's use of scripted questions throughout the play in developing the narrative, characters and perspective. How does this impact on the audience?

+ Discuss how the skills demonstrated both in and out of role could be transferred to analytical responses about the writer's techniques and the effect on the audience.

+ Analyse how the language devices and techniques are used to explore:
    + Characters
    + Relationships
    + Power
    + A sense of voice
    + Tension

7. Playwroughting

To explore the dramatic techniques and language choices used by the playwright in a specific scene.

Learning

✦ As a class, read the following extracts from page 68 and pages 72–74

From Christopher kneels down.

to A Ticket Collector stops him.

And

From Are you for real?

to Count the trains. Figure it out. Get the rhythm right.

Teaching & Resources

▣ Before beginning this, activity discuss the origin of the word playwright as described by Simon Stephens in a *Guardian* interview.

'Stephens thinks he has gained much from adapting the novel. "Having to put text on stage is good exercise. I just think it made me a better writer: it nourished me intellectually." He doesn't think of himself as a writer, he says, but a "wroughter: the 'wright' in playwright comes from to wrought rather than to write". Writing adaptations is a better means of honing his craft than writing for TV or film would be, he argues. And these ideas of nourishment and honing are becoming more important to him as he gets older. It is helpful to project the text and have

♦ Working in groups of 4 to 6 pupils, you will be given a section of the play taken from the extracts you have just read.

♦ Choose who will take on the role of each character in the extract. In addition, one student will represent the playwright.

♦ You will produce a Digital Video Clip of your extract but this time you will freeze the action at two significant points. These should be identified as moments when the actors need to understand or know something that the playwright has to answer or explain.

♦ As you Action Read the extract, the playwright stands at the side of the action. When the Action is frozen, the 'actor' who needs to ask the question steps forward and completes the sentence, 'As you are the playwright I need to ask . . . '

♦ The student representing the playwright will then step forward and respond by answering the question and/or explaining the technique used.

individual copies of the texts for the students.'

The numbers in the class will determine the size of the extracts. The extracts are deliberately short.

You might suggest that the actors clap their hands to distinguish the moments when the Action Reading needs to freeze.

As the groups are working on these extracts, questions and responses, ensure that you go round the class, providing advice and discussing the dramatic techniques and writer's aims.

- Continue this process until the extract is complete and your group has frozen two times and asked/answered two questions.

- All the students who have represented the playwright in their groups now form a new group in the centre of the circle, to represent the Playwright communally as one group. In the centre of this new group will be placed a card with Playwright clearly printed on it. While the groups of actors continue to rehearse their Action Readings, frozen moments and questions, the 'Playwright' group discuss the questions they have been asked and share ideas on how to best answer them.

At this stage, you will probably work with the 'Playwright' group to ensure that they are confident about discussing and responding to the questions. You may also have deliberately selected the students who take on this collective role.

- As a class, produce your Digital Video Clips as Rolling Theatre. All the groups freeze in their initial Still Image and then the first group 'comes to life' and begins their Action Reading. At the first significant moment, they freeze, the actor steps forward and completes the sentence, 'As you are the playwright I need to ask . . . ' so that everyone in the class can hear.

The teacher can intervene at this stage to assist with the playwright group's responses if necessary.

- The 'Playwrights' discuss (loudly enough for everyone to hear) the question/issue, as if considering the idea within the playwright's head, and then respond. The Action Reading continues until the next significant moment when the process is repeated. When the first group has completed their Digital Video Clip and freezes, the next group knows that they can begin. This process continues with all the groups producing their Digital Video Clips, asking the questions and hearing the 'Playwright' group's thoughts and responses, until all groups have shown their pieces and all the questions have been discussed.

Further activities, reflection, analysis or discussion

- Discuss, and evidence, the dramatic techniques and theatrical devices identified above. How do these devices influence our understanding of the narrative, characters and ideas? Does this differ from the influences that the novelist has, through the techniques he uses?

8. Distancing the audience

To develop an understanding of alienation techniques used by the playwright and analyse the effect on the audience.

Learning	Teaching & Resources
✦ Remaining in the groups used for the last activity, stand in a large circle with sight of the projected text. Each group has been given a large card with the word 'Audience' printed on it. Read the opening of the extract from pages 96 and 97 where Christopher is sitting his A Level Exam,	▣ It is helpful to project the text
	✐ Props – several large pieces of card with Audience printed on them.
Christopher I can see the questions but I can't read the questions because when I look at the words they all seem confused and the wrong way round and mixed up to me.	
Rev Peters Right.	
Christopher What does this question say?	
Rev Peters Christopher, I'm afraid I can't help you like that. I'm not allowed to.	
✦ Sculpt the characters of Christopher and Rev Peters in to the scene at this point in the play.	✐ Props – exam paper.

- As a group, decide where to Place the Audience and position your card in the agreed place. You need to consider which character the audience empathises with, whose eyes they might be looking through, how close they feel to the situation etc. The teacher will ask you to justify your positioning of the audience using evidence from the text.

- The sculpted characters continue to Action Read the extract, pausing after each speech, so that the groups can move their 'Audience' cards and justify the positions that they take up.

- When Siobhan speaks, she will need to be sculpted into or near the scene and when she says the following line you will need to think carefully about what impact this has on the positioning of the audience and why.

  Christopher, people won't want to hear about the answer to a maths question in a play.

- Continue the process of the sculpted characters Action Reading and freezing after each speech so that the Audience can be Placed and the positioning

Props – several large pieces of card with Audience printed on them.

Use targeted questioning to explore the groups' positioning of the audience and their justification. Encourage them to use specific evidence from the text to support their comments.

At this stage, you might want to discuss in more detail the Brechtian idea of alienation, where the playwright, through a variety of techniques, deliberately keeps the audience conscious of the fact that it is a theatrical performance. Discuss why a playwright might want the audience to respond to what they are watching on stage in a distanced, objective way.

discussed. This continues until the speech,

> **Rev Peters** I'll have a quick word with the big man for you. And let's see what happens, shall we?

✦ The sculpted characters freeze and the teacher reads the comment from Mark Haddon.

'Christopher is an outsider, and novelists are drawn to outsiders of all kinds because they grant us a privileged position from which we are able to look back at ourselves.'

Discuss this quotation with the class.

Further activities, reflection, analysis or discussion

✦ Discuss the dramatic techniques and theatrical devices used to control the audience's relationship with the characters on stage. How do these devices influence our understanding of the narrative, characters and ideas? Does this differ from the influences that the novelist has, through the techniques he used?

✦ When placing the audience are you influenced by the techniques the playwright uses and/or by your own experiences in life and your ability to relate to particular characters and/or ideas? How might this process affect the way we approach and understood Simon Stephens' adaptation of the novel?

9. Truth and lies

To re-examine the significance of the quotations used in the first activity.

Learning

✦ Before this last activity, you will need to think carefully about all the activities you have been involved in and re-read the quotations around the room and the evidence and recorded ideas placed in envelopes.

✦ As a class, sit in a large semi-circle facing the projected quotations and discuss what they now mean and what significance they have.

✦ Look at the projected image of a Venn diagram and discuss which words or ideas suggested by either quotation could now be placed in the central overlap area in the Venn diagram? Why?

✦ The teacher will place two large hoops on the floor to create a new Venn diagram and hand out individual pieces of card. After thinking about all the activities and techniques explored, write a quotation or idea, on the piece of card, that you feel is particularly significant to the play.

Teaching & Resources

🖙 Props – quotations, envelopes, recorded ideas.

'The word metaphor means carrying something from one place to another and it is when you describe something by using a word for something that it isn't' and 'I don't like acting because it is pretending that something is real when it is not really real at all so it is like a kind of lie'.

▣ Project the quotations.

🖙 Props – pieces of card, large hoops/circles of string to create a Venn diagram on the floor.

- As a class, sit in a large circle around with the Venn diagram in the centre. The teacher labels the Venn diagram as Truth and Lies. Working round the circle one at a time, place your quotation or idea in the Venn diagram where you feel it is best placed, reading it aloud as you do so.

- Once all the cards have been placed, the teacher will read,

  Christopher No. I don't like acting because it is pretending that something is real when it is not really real at all so it is like a kind of lie.

  Siobhan But people like stories, Christopher. Some people find things which are kind of true in things which are made up.

▣ Project a Venn diagram.

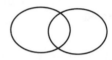

▣ Project the text.

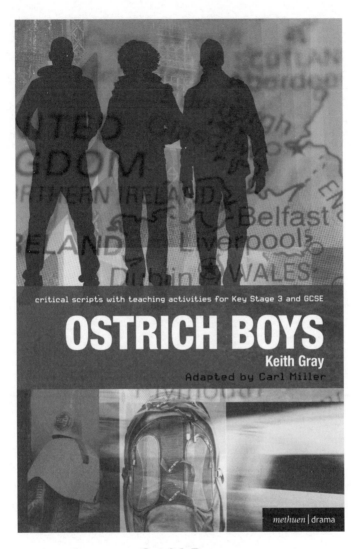

Ostrich Boys
by Keith Gray, adapted for the stage by Carl Miller

*Three friends, an urn containing the ashes of their best friend, and
261 miles to give him the send-off he deserves: this play edition
of Keith Gray's terrific novel is a sure-fire hit.*

ISBN 978 1 408 1 3082 7

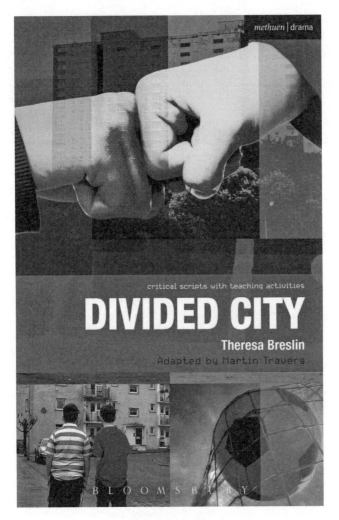

Divided City

by Theresa Breslin, adapted for the stage by Martin Travers

*What could be more important than football? In a city divided
by sectarianism two boys are united by a secret pact to help
an asylum seeker and his girlfriend. A gripping new drama
adapted from Theresa Breslin's hit novel.*

ISBN 978 1 4081 8157 7